# *Making* DISCIPLES

# *Making* DISCIPLES

## *A Tool for the Christian Disciple-Maker*

*Benjamin Gum*

SOUL PURPOSE PUBLISHING
Books & Music

ISBN 978-1-7344962-0-8

Soul Purpose Publishing
Shawnee, KS

# Contents

# Preface

Jesus commanded his disciples to make disciples. I presume that is why you are reading this right now. You are a disciple who follows Jesus, and you want to be obedient and make more of the same. Pause at the end of this sentence and worship God for even that desire, for "it is God who is working in you both to will and to work according to his good purpose" (Phi 2:13).

To "make disciples" is so broad a charge that many volumes could not fully describe what it looks like. The process enfolds the earliest of pre-evangelistic phases to the very last acts of dying well as a mature saint. Any one disciple-maker may find oneself participating anywhere along that line of another's faith journey, perhaps for a brief time, perhaps for the whole stretch. And making disciples looks different in every case, though the gospel truths through which each transformation happens are always the same. One disciple needs more learning while another knows a lot but needs more accountability for obedience. One has never heard the gospel before you shared it while another has heard it hundreds of times in church gatherings. One seems well on the way in a few short weeks while another needs intense care and support many months later.

It is both the potential scope and diversity of making disciples that makes it nearly impossible to offer a disciple-maker one tool and send them off. Even the one tool of Scripture requires the Helper, the Holy Spirit, if it is to be of any use. So, it is reasonable to expect one should accumulate many good tools over time as a disciple-maker, tools that help access the Bible itself and make sense of it, and tools that draw from the Scriptures to offer practical steps for obedience.

My first goal is to give you a very basic tool. I hope to help you walk through the most fundamental aspects of what a disciple of Jesus is and does. What must they know at a bare minimum? How should they live?

I grew up in the church but never had any one person intentionally take me aside for disciple-making one-on-one or in a targeted small group, like Jesus did with the Twelve or especially with Peter, James and John. At least, if that was someone's intention, I was not aware of it. Like many, I was discipled to some extent by Christian parents and youth pastors, but not really taken on as a project for targeted growth. I was more like one in the crowds: "discipleship by the village," you could say. Large group disciple-making is important, gathering to sing the Word together, to pray it, to hear it taught, to live it out in the giving of gifts and in the ordinances of baptism and communion. But I have come to see the high value of prayerfully seeking out one or two or a few at a time to meet with to train and encourage in maturing faith. And I want to help you do that. What's more, I want to help you then help someone else do that.

I pray God blesses your willingness to minister in this way, and that he blesses this tool to that end.

Benjamin Gum

# Acknowledgements

May all the glory go to God for any good that comes from this resource. For his sake, I hope that turns out to be *much* good. Thanks to my Lord Jesus for life in his name, and for the gifts he expresses through me to build his church.

Profound thanks to my amazing wife, Dawna, who repeatedly encouraged me to create a written tool for disciple-making. There are many such resources, but you finally convinced me I should craft my own offering for the church. On occasions when I am 99% convinced God is moving in my own mind, he seems to speak through your voice to give me that last nudge I need. I can't recall ever regretting letting you talk me into such things. This time was no exception.

Thanks also to those in my family and church circles who helped me refine this work so it might be of better use for those who want to make disciples: Tim and Nicole Houser; Jake and Jes Ronning; Dave and Katie Reimer; Phil and Jill Pettis; Doug and Nancy Carlson; Ron Bennett, Linda Wilson, Virginia Hawk and others.

# Introduction

You are reading this resource as a direct result of the one command that Christ gave to his disciples that is the mandate around which all their activities are focused. It is recorded in Matthew 28, and it anchors in one word: *disciple*. We tend to read that as a noun, but in this command, it is a verb translated, "make disciples."

The command, usually called the Great Commission, is in vv.19-20, but the narrative section clearly begins at v.16, and these preceding verses provide important context. Let us look at the text and make a few observations.

> Matthew 28:16–20 (CSB)
>
> 16 The eleven disciples traveled to Galilee, to the mountain where
> Jesus had directed them. 17 When they saw him, they worshiped, but
> some doubted. 18 Jesus came near and said to them, "All authority
> has been given to me in heaven and on earth. 19 Go, therefore, and
> make disciples of all nations, baptizing them in the name of the
> Father and of the Son and of the Holy Spirit, 20 teaching them to
> observe everything I have commanded you. And remember, I am with you always, to the end of the age."

First, notice disciples are characterized by obedience to Jesus' commands (v.16). Jesus told them to meet him, and they did as he directed them. Second, notice disciples are characterized by worshiping Jesus – even in spite of doubts (v.17). Notice, too, that worshiping Jesus follows seeing Jesus. Obeying Jesus, seeing Jesus and worshiping Jesus are marks of disciples. Obeying him puts them in position to see him and respond in worship. (It is also true that seeing Jesus leads to worship expressed in obedience.)

Then Jesus declares his ultimate authority in every realm. This authority is bound up in the reason for the worship and provides the answer to the doubts. Disciples are under the authority of Jesus. Authority to do what? Here is the command: make disciples. Make them everywhere at all times from all peoples. How? The way Jesus did. Identifying them with himself through baptism (this will be explained more fully later on) and teaching them to observe his commands. Please note the text does not say, "...teaching them everything I have commanded you." It is not less than that, but it is more: "teaching them *to observe* everything I have commanded you." Making disciples necessarily involves teaching, but to merely accept that teaching intellectually – a submission of the mind – does not make one a disciple. That requires obedience, the submission of the will. The baptism is a symbolic declaration of one's will to be a disciple and the obedience that comes through teaching is the follow-through, the worship of Jesus through continued submission.

The sustaining presence and power of Christ is what enables the disciple himself or herself to endure in this mission, and it is also what enables the disciple to make more disciples (v.20). Jesus has the authority and does the work of making disciples. But he does that work through his disciples. And he will sustain that work until he returns at the end of this age.

So, the task is to make disciples. How might this tool help? It is my goal that this resource will be useful whether you meet with someone who is not yet a follower of Christ or with someone who has been a follower for any amount of time. A seeker needs to understand the essentials of what a disciple of Jesus is and does in order to decide to become one. A new disciple needs to grow in understanding of and obedience to Christ's commands. And even the one who has been a disciple for a long time (including the one in the disciple-making role) needs to rehearse gospel truths to avoid the ditches of legalism and license as he or she continues to worship Christ in thanksgiving through obedient and holy living.

This resource will address the essentials for disciples of Jesus, and essentially follow our key observations from Matthew's text. First, we will begin with who Jesus is and why he is worthy of worship, obedience and all authority. Next, we will consider who his disciples are, and how they are made as they are being restored to what God intended all humans to be. Then, we will dig into what disciples do as they learn to observe everything Jesus commanded.

This tool is intended to flex with your needs as you make disciples. If you need to slow down and dwell on part of a chapter, do so. If you are best served covering a couple of chapters in one meeting, that is great too. If it is helpful to take the time to read every Scripture reference, do so. But if you are meeting with someone who is familiar with a reference and needs only reminded of its content, that's great! If you best serve a disciple – or a potential one – by suspending your use of this text and digging into a portion of Scripture or another resource, then by all means do what is most helpful. I will even make some suggestions along those lines as we go.

My goal is to provide a basic main street for covering disciple-making essentials and suggest a few related cul-de-sacs that may be worth visiting along the way.

Blessings as you proceed!

# Part One: Who Is Jesus?

Imagine you are looking for employment. You have sifted through companies and job openings hoping to find a match for your skills, passions and needs. You have just arrived at the location for one of your top prospects and are awaiting an interview. You watch the hustle and bustle of this company at work: employees here and there, performing various tasks, and a few individuals you identify as supervisors or bosses based on their dress, demeanor and interactions with employees.

In walks a man you had not yet seen. Everyone seems to take notice and sharpen up. He's well-dressed, all-business but friendly enough and you can sense he has everyone's attention by default. *Who is this guy? He must be the CEO or maybe the owner or both! He is awesome! Whomever he is, I want to be like that!*

This scene captures the essence of what we want to grasp in Part One of this book. To become a disciple of Jesus, or to grow as his disciple, we must know him and cherish him and must continue to grow in both knowing and cherishing him. This is because the disciple's goal is to be more and more like him. To consider what being a disciple of Jesus is and does, we need to understand and revere the boss, so to speak. *Who is this guy? Why do his disciples follow him, obey him and even WORSHIP him?*

To answer those questions about Jesus, we have to back up a bit – well, actually all the way to the beginning. First, let's just briefly summarize the part leading up to Jesus.

The first century Jewish community had a history of encounters with Yahweh, the one who identified himself to them as the one true God (Ex 3:13-15). These encounters were recorded in the Old Testament (OT) portion of what we now call the Bible. Also recorded were the covenants God made with these descendants of Abraham to bless all peoples through them (Gn 12:1-3; 17:3-14,19,21; 28:13-14; 2 Sam 7:8-16). God gave them rules to live by, so that they could draw near to his presence and so they could show his greatness and glory to all other peoples (Dt 26:16-19). The OT records failure after failure by these Hebrews to live up to God's standards, though God himself was always only perfectly faithful, patient and merciful. He knew his people would fail.

That's why he told his people that he was going to send someone appointed to the task of rescuing them (Psa 2; Dan 7:13-14; Is 9:2-7; 52:13-53:12). This Appointed One, or Messiah, would do more than lead them to national greatness. He would save them from their repeated failures – their *sins*. He himself would be righteous and would bring them back into right standing with God. God would replace their stony hearts – unable to obey – with new hearts (Ezek 11:19; 36:26). What's more, this appointed Servant would bring blessing to those of *every* people group.

*Who would this Messiah be? When would he come? And how would he save them?*

In ch.1, we will briefly explore how God (Yahweh) reveals himself, revealed his glory to us and especially how he revealed himself prior to the first century, for this sets up our understanding of who Jesus is. Then in ch.2, we will discover that the very nature of God presents an obstacle for us. He is far beyond our capacities to know. He is also too good for us to approach. Last, in ch.3, we will see how everything God had already revealed about himself relates to Jesus, who shook the world like nobody before or since! In Jesus we'll find the solution to the problem of our unworthiness to approach God. We'll also see that what God revealed in Jesus he continues to reveal through his disciples who follow after him.

# Ch.1 Revelation

## Knowing God through His Creation

God has revealed himself to us, has shown his greatness and glory. This is perhaps the most fundamental tenet of Christianity. In the most basic sense God has revealed himself to us through his creation. We are aware of ourselves and of our surroundings, and we possess the ability to draw reasonable conclusions about what we observe. We all have a built-in sense of an ultimate reality far beyond us, beyond our limited view of time, space and matter. The word "God" is at minimum used to define that ultimate reality.

Sound rational thinking leads us naturally to further conclude that God is the single most excellent being that is supremely powerful, knowledgeable and good. This God is the answer to the so-called First Cause – the reason why something exists rather than nothing. He is the explanation why all people groups everywhere have a basic moral code, holding some activities as evil and punishable, such as torturing of small children or premeditated murder. He is the explanation behind cravings, and why nothing in this life seems to satisfy our desires completely or perpetually.

We all sense there is a God. We might try to rename or redefine him – even as an "it" – but we all know. Some want very much to believe the ultimate reality is stuff, that matter is what is eternal and ultimate. That doesn't explain morality nor answer the First Cause problem. Some want to believe in many gods but that is irrational for multiple things cannot be ultimate.

God has hard-wired his creatures to be aware of him. Even broken creatures retain that built-in sense that he exists. Just like we may be alone in a room, and then without hearing or seeing someone enter may somehow be aware they came in, God has given us a sense of his presence.

**Talk it over:**

*What alternate worldviews (perspectives) have you heard offered to explain what is the ultimate reality of the universe?*

*Is there any alternative to God as the ultimate reality that is a MORE reasonable explanation for what we observe in the world? Why or why not?*

*If there is a God, one that is supremely good, would it make sense to expect that he would reveal himself to his creatures? Why or why not?*

## Knowing God through His Word

In the first section of this chapter, I deliberately avoided any references from Scripture (the Bible). I wanted to make that first point from its own natural perspective. Many brilliant thinkers have constructed rock solid arguments that lead rationally to the ultimate reality as God. God at this point is identified as perfection in power, knowledge and goodness. This is the farthest one can get with what is called *general revelation*, that is, the degree to which we can know God through natural observation alone. There is much more to know about God, and more than that, there is much more to *knowing* God.

Picture yourself (if it is not actually the case) as a teenager. You look forward to one day soon meeting that special someone. You know your future spouse is out there, and they are awesome! You imagine what they are like, every best expression of the characteristics for which you are looking in a mate. You watch for them in every situation – *is this the one?*

At some point, you finally meet them. You are introduced. You learn their name and everything you can about them. They are in some ways exactly what you expected, and in other ways not at all.

This is a rough picture of getting to know God. From general revelation we can know what he must be. This is more than what we *hope* to find in a spouse, because we understand they will not be the ultimate best of everything. But with God, he *must* be. That tells us a lot, but it doesn't tell us his name. It doesn't give us a personal relationship with him. We can only know something *about* him, but we can't *know* him.

That's where *special revelation* comes in. God has revealed himself generally through his amazing, beautiful creation and through the built-in awareness he gave us, but he has given us more. He has given us a special revelation of himself, more detailed and more personal. And this is how we not only know more *about* him, but how we come to *know* him.

We know God through his Word. Later on, we'll see another aspect of this Word, but at this point, I mean the Bible, the supernatural book that God guided a number of men over a period of centuries to write according to his design. God worked through these writers' personalities, languages and settings to breathe out for us what is the most brilliant literary work of all time and is his divinely orchestrated presentation of himself to all mankind. It records the beginning of his creative work all the way through to the culmination of his rescue plan, all of human history and future and more. It tells us his name. It teaches us truths about him, and shows how he works, even at times revealing a glimpse of his heavenly perspective and activity (e.g., Job 1-2). It shows us how to draw near to him, to actually *know* him.

It is the Bible that explains what we sense intuitively. Through it we understand why we are drawn to think deeply about big things (Ecc. 3:11). It tells us not just about God but helps us know ourselves and one another better. It affirms and explains what we already said about general revelation, and then carries us so much deeper. God has more than hard-wired us to know that he exists. He has given us the Bible so that we may know him.

**Talk it over:**
Read Rm 1:18-23...

> 18 For God's wrath is revealed from heaven against all
> godlessness and unrighteousness of people who by their
> unrighteousness suppress the truth, 19 since what can be known
> about God is evident among them, because God has shown it to
> them. 20 For his invisible attributes, that is, his eternal power and
> divine nature, have been clearly seen since the creation of the world,
> being understood through what he has made. As a result, people are
> without excuse. 21 For though they knew God, they did not glorify
> him as God or show gratitude. Instead, their thinking became
> worthless, and their senseless hearts were darkened. 22 Claiming to
> be wise, they became fools 23 and exchanged the glory of the

immortal God for images resembling mortal man, birds, four-footed animals, and reptiles. (CSB)

*How does this passage explain what we discussed about general revelation on p.4?*

*How does our built-in sense of morality relate to v.18?*

*What does it mean in v.20 that people are without excuse?*

*In spite of God's revelation to mankind in creation, what is man's natural response in these verses?*

Read 2 Pt 1:20-21...

> [20] Above all, you know this: No prophecy of Scripture comes
> from the prophet's own interpretation, [21] because no prophecy ever
> came by the will of man; instead, men spoke from God as they were
> carried along by the Holy Spirit.

Read 2 Tm 3:15-17...

> [15] and you know that from infancy you have known the sacred
> Scriptures, which are able to give you wisdom for salvation through
> faith in Christ Jesus. [16] All Scripture is inspired by God and is
> profitable for teaching, for rebuking, for correcting, for training in
> righteousness, [17] so that the man of God may be complete, equipped
> for every good work. (CSB)

*What do these verses tell us about the origin of Scripture (the Bible)?*

*Why does this set the Bible apart as unique and trustworthy?*

*How does this relate to our definition of God, especially to his ultimate knowledge and goodness?*

*How does Paul in vv.16-17 say God's revelation through the Bible is important for a disciple (the "man of God")?*

*How important then is the Bible to a disciple, and how would you expect the disciple to respond to that reality?*

## Knowing God through His Spirit

God has revealed himself through his Word, the Bible. The good news is that this means we can actually know God. Remember, that is the foundation for a disciple – to know and revere and cherish the one he or she follows. As we read earlier in 2 Tm 3:15, this truth can save our lives. The bad news is the problem mentioned by Paul in Rm 1. Even with the Bible in front of us – even if we were to read the whole thing! – our natural response to God is ungodly living that suppresses the truth, robs him of his glory and distorts our thinking so we can't know him, and we worship anything else instead. Paul's point is, that's on *us*. It's not God's fault but our own. So, how then can we get past our ungodliness and distorted thinking to know God? Through his Spirit.

God's Spirit, often called the Holy Spirit, is the Person through which God reaches out to our own mind and spirit. This Spirit is fully and exactly God himself, and though we will not see him, he makes it possible for us to know God. He opens our minds to get past our distorted thinking and truly understand what God has shown us in the Bible (1 Cor 2:6-16). He wakes our spirits up from death so we can begin living for God (Ezek 37:14; Jn 6:63; Rm 8:10-11), and he lives within us as the most intimate expression of the God we desire to know.

Knowing God is only possible through the Spirit and the Word, but everyone does not come to know God. This also requires work on the part of Jesus which we will discuss later. For now, the point is that God reveals himself through his Spirit to awaken man's spirit to understand and believe

God's revelation through his Word. Becoming a disciple of Jesus depends on this revelation.

Think back to the analogy of the eager anticipation to meet your future spouse. Imagine you had not yet met the one you hoped to marry, but he or she had sent you a bunch of love letters written in a code you could not understand. You had both imagined and heard wonderful things about your love that you knew were contained in the letters. You were dying to understand them!

Then one day you get a phone call. It is the one you love. You now interact in a conversation in real time, and you are elated as they explain everything. The letters are made clear, and the words do in fact fill your heart with joy and life. What's more, just the sound of their voice floods you with love and your heart races as though you were face-to-face!

That's something like how God is known through his Word and his Spirit, though the analogy falls short. With the Holy Spirit, God's actual presence is with you, not just his voice. And when someone does come to life this way and becomes a disciple of Jesus, the Holy Spirit gives them an ongoing inward confidence of that presence and that relationship with God (Rm 8:12-17).

**Talk it over**

Read the words of Jesus in Jn 16:13-15...

> 13 When the Spirit of truth comes, he will guide you into all the truth. For he will not speak on his own, but he will speak whatever he hears. He will also declare to you what is to come. 14 He will glorify me, because he will take from what is mine and declare it to you. 15 Everything the Father has is mine. This is why I told you that he takes from what is mine and will declare it to you.

*How has God's Spirit opened your eyes to something you didn't understand before?*

*When have you sensed God's presence in a particularly strong way?*

*How have you been surprised by something God has shown you about himself?*

*Thinking back to our analogies, how is getting to know God like meeting your future spouse? How is it different?*

*How is it like meeting your new boss? How is it different?*

**Pray and Worship**

Take a moment together to worship God for his perfect excellence in every way. To pray is to talk with God. To worship is to humble yourself before him and declare his ultimate worth, like a subject would bow before a king. Humbly talk to God together and declare his greatness. You might even use some of his own words from Scriptures in this chapter – what better words than his own! Thank him that he in his goodness and love has revealed himself to you in his creation and through his Word. Thank him especially for sending his Spirit to give you the most intimate sense of his presence.

# Ch.2 The Roadblock of Holiness

In ch.1 we discussed the need for the Holy Spirit to overcome our problem of distorted thinking that comes from our ungodliness. This problem is a roadblock in the most profound way to our knowing God – far more than a mere intellectual obstruction. Our ungodly attitudes and actions – our sins – disqualify us entirely from God's presence. How can we know God if we can't even come near him?

Let's take our analogy from ch.1 – the one where we excitedly look for that special someone – and imagine it in a familiar setting:

> *You are in a large high school cafeteria full of classmates. You have already identified someone you hope could be that special someone, and you have been crushing on them big time! You finish grabbing your food, and turn around with your tray in hand, looking for a place to sit. Suddenly, there they are! Your heart threatens to pound right out of your chest. They are so amazing! You want so badly to go sit next to them and just take in their awesomeness! Then you realize you have a problem. They are so wonderful you couldn't possibly go sit at their table. And they are surrounded by the best sorts of people. You don't belong there. You couldn't possibly fit in. This is hopeless!*

Well, we realize when that kind of scene plays out among other mere humans (all too often in our church gatherings!), our perceptions are *exaggerated* often to the point of silliness, especially when it happens among teenagers. However, with God the reality is infinitely *understated.* Once we finally get a glimpse of God's amazing beauty and glory, we realize we couldn't possibly sit at his table. We are right to think that. The reason is holiness.

We already discussed the essence of holiness, that God is utterly *unique* in his excellence. Another crucial aspect of his holiness is his *purity*. Because his nature is the perfection of goodness, anything that falls short of that perfection cannot survive the nearness of his presence. This is why most of the time when God makes a personal appearance (called a *theophany*) before a human, they do not expect to survive it. I understand that a little bit.

When I was about twelve years old, growing up in South Central Kansas, we had a thunderstorm hit. That wasn't unusual. But on this occasion, I realized I had forgotten to turn off the lights in our detached workshop. I headed out to turn them off, crossing the thirty or so feet from our back porch to the shop door amidst gusty winds, rain and the strobe effect of lightning against a dark sky. I was about half way into the doorway when BOOM! – lightning struck a big old elm tree that stood only twenty feet away. I hit the floor.

First, I thought I was dead. Then, though still stunned, I decided I was only deaf. Finally, after a minute or two, the shock wore off. I started to once again hear the wind and rain and distant thunder, and I realized I was fine. The tree, however, was forever scarred.

Imagine the danger of coming near to the one who *makes* lightning! Talk about hitting the ground! We have concluded he is good – we had better hope so! But it turns out that God's goodness is actually our biggest problem. He *is* good. And we are *not*. That means drawing near to him is far more dangerous than coming near a tall tree in a thunderstorm.

The Hebrews of the OT – the people to whom God revealed himself and to whom he gave his Word – they understood God's holiness and the dangerous implications. God had warned Moses from a mysterious burning shrub that even the ground near himself was holy (Ex 3:5). And later when the LORD prepared to deliver his law to them, the scene where he came down on Mount Sinai was far more terrible than a Kansas thunderstorm:

Exodus 19:16–22

> **16** On the third day, when morning came, there was thunder and lightning, a thick cloud on the mountain, and a very loud trumpet sound, so that all the people in the camp shuddered. **17** Then Moses brought the people out of the camp to meet God, and they stood at the foot of the mountain. **18** Mount Sinai was completely enveloped in smoke because the LORD came down on it in fire. Its smoke went up like the smoke of a furnace, and the whole mountain shook violently. **19** As the sound of the trumpet grew louder and louder, Moses spoke and God answered him in the thunder.
>
> **20** The LORD came down on Mount Sinai at the top of the mountain. Then the LORD summoned Moses to the top of the mountain, and he went

up. 21 The LORD directed Moses, "Go down and warn the people not to
break through to see the LORD; otherwise many of them will die. 22 Even
the priests who come near the LORD must consecrate themselves, or the
LORD will break out in anger against them."

God's holiness is a big deal. This is infinitely more serious than standing red-faced in a lunchroom or hitting the ground near a lightning strike. Approaching him in our natural state is a death sentence. Two essential things shown in the short narrative above must take place if we are to survive encountering God. First, notice the LORD summoned Moses (v.20). That is essentially the work we talked about in ch.1 that the Holy Spirit does. He draws and invites us to God, awakens us and makes the meeting possible. Second, those who come near must "consecrate themselves" (v.22). At its core, this expresses the idea of preparation through purification. God's people become impure (unholy) through sin and even through routine and inadvertent contact with things associated with death. They must be purified. Otherwise, meeting with God will be walking into a lightning bolt.

This is the reason God was meeting with Moses on the mountain. It was to give him the law for his people, a code of conduct that showed them how to prepare to draw near to him. That law provided a system of ceremony that enacted the purifying of God's people through obedience and faith in what God would do to fix their sinfulness. The system itself did not accomplish this, but it pointed to a reality that would one day solve the problem forever.

The writer of the Hebrews (the NT book to Hebrew Christians) referenced this OT scene as he affirmed the gravity of God's holiness and the importance of purification through faith in Jesus, whose blood makes it possible for every one of his disciples to draw near to God:

Hebrews 12:14–29

14 Pursue peace with everyone, and holiness—without it no one will
see the Lord. 15 Make sure that no one falls short of the grace of God and
that no root of bitterness springs up, causing trouble and defiling many.
16 And make sure that there isn't any immoral or irreverent person like
Esau, who sold his birthright in exchange for a single meal. 17 For you
know that later, when he wanted to inherit the blessing, he was rejected,

even though he sought it with tears, because he didn't find any
opportunity for repentance.

18 For you have not come to what could be touched, to a blazing fire,
to darkness, gloom, and storm, 19 to the blast of a trumpet, and the sound
of words. Those who heard it begged that not another word be spoken to
them, 20 for they could not bear what was commanded: **If even an
animal touches the mountain, it must be stoned.**, 21 The
appearance was so terrifying that Moses said, **I am trembling with
fear.**, 22 Instead, you have come to Mount Zion, to the city of the living
God (the heavenly Jerusalem), to myriads of angels, a festive gathering,
23 to the assembly of the firstborn whose names have been written in
heaven, to a Judge, who is God of all, to the spirits of righteous people
made perfect, 24 and to Jesus, the mediator of a new covenant, and to the
sprinkled blood, which says better things than the blood of Abel.

25 See to it that you do not reject the one who speaks. For if they did
not escape when they rejected him who warned them on earth, even less
will we if we turn away from him who warns us from heaven. 26 His voice
shook the earth at that time, but now he has promised, **Yet once more
I will shake not only the earth but also the heavens.**, 27 This
expression, "Yet once more," indicates the removal of what can be
shaken—that is, created things—so that what is not shaken might
remain. 28 Therefore, since we are receiving a kingdom that cannot be
shaken, let us be thankful. By it, we may serve God acceptably, with
reverence and awe, 29 for our God is a consuming fire.

Jesus is the one who provides the "holiness without [which] no one will see the Lord." He and his disciples will be the focus of ch.3, where we will see how God reveals himself through his Son and through those who follow him.

God's holiness is both what makes knowing him supremely desirable and utterly impossible – apart from Jesus. Unless God graciously bridged the gap and made a way for us to become holy as he is holy (Eph 1:4; 1 Pt 1:15), we could never sit at his table, could never come work for him or represent him, could never approach him or survive his presence. This matter of God's holiness is life or death, because one day everyone will either be forevermore in God's presence or forevermore banished from it. The former is the definition of life while the latter is the definition of death.

For a brilliant video resource on God's holiness go to thebibleproject.com.

**Talk it over**

*When was a time you were excluded from some person or group because you or others felt you were "unworthy?"*

*Why were those feelings valid or invalid?*

*When have you been most struck by God's greatness? How did that awareness make you feel?*

*Why should we feel unworthy to know or even approach God in our natural sinful state?*

*What kind or amount of sin does it take to violate God's perfect holiness?*

*If you have never trusted God to give you his own purifying holiness through Jesus' blood sacrifice, will you do so now?*

(Ask for help if you don't quite understand or know what to do.)

**Pray and Worship**

Praise God for his perfect holiness. In the Bible, praise means a sort of bubbling over, an overflow. The idea is that one is so filled with wonder at God's beauty, majesty and power that it cannot be contained and must be expressed outwardly. Those outward expressions are praise. It is something like the way proud parents erupt in cheers for their children at a graduation, a sporting event, a concert, etc. God is the one who is ultimately praiseworthy simply because of who he is, so brag on him, cheer for him, be amazed and say what is true about him. Then thank him for providing through Jesus the holiness without which you could never see the Lord.

Songs can be very helpful to express praise to God. Consider these lyrics from an old worship hymn, and if you know them, you might sing them now in worship:

**Holy, Holy, Holy**
*Holy, holy, holy, Lord God Almighty*
*Early in the morning our song shall rise to Thee*
*Holy, holy, holy, merciful and mighty*
*God in three Persons, blessed Trinity*

*Holy, holy, holy, all the saints adore Thee*
*Casting down their golden crowns around the glassy sea*
*Cherubim and seraphim falling down before Thee*
*Which wert and art and evermore shalt be*

*Holy, holy, holy, though the darkness hide Thee*
*Though the eye of sinful man thy glory may not see*
*Only Thou art holy; there is none beside Thee*
*Perfect in pow'r, in love and purity*

*Holy, holy, holy, Lord God Almighty*
*All Thy works shall praise Thy name in earth and sky and sea*
*Holy, holy, holy, merciful and mighty*
*God in three Persons, blessed Trinity*

# Ch.3 Incarnation

We have established that to be a disciple starts with coming to know God. We saw that we all have a built-in sense that God exists, and a craving that will only be satisfied by knowing him. This is more than knowing *about* him. It is *knowing* him and being known *by* him (Gal 4:8). We discussed that this kind of knowledge only happens through God's self-revelation through his Word, the Bible, as our minds and spirits are awakened to God through his Holy Spirit. But coming into a relationship with God in the most intimate way, the only way that leads to eternal life, comes through his ultimate revelation to us – his *incarnation*. That's a theological term that refers to God's taking on human form through the Eternal Son, Jesus.

## Knowing God through His Son

Beyond the written Scriptures, the incarnation expresses the fullest sense of the Word of God. The Apostle John uses that language to begin his gospel showing that Jesus is God's full revelation of himself to us in human flesh:

John 1:1–18

**1** In the beginning was the Word, and the Word was with God, and
the Word was God. 2 He was with God in the beginning. 3 All things were
created through him, and apart from him not one thing was created that
has been created. 4 In him was life, and that life was the light of men.
5 That light shines in the darkness, and yet the darkness did not
overcome it.

6 There was a man sent from God whose name was John. 7 He came
as a witness to testify about the light, so that all might believe through
him. 8 He was not the light, but he came to testify about the light.

9 The true light that gives light to everyone, was coming into the
world.

10 He was in the world, and the world was created through him, and
yet the world did not recognize him. 11 He came to his own, and his own

people did not receive him. 12 But to all who did receive him, he gave them the right to be children of God, to those who believe in his name, 13 who were born, not of natural descent, or of the will of the flesh, or of the will of man, but of God.

14 The Word became flesh and dwelt among us. We observed his glory, the glory as the one and only Son from the Father, full of grace and truth. 15 (John testified concerning him and exclaimed, "This was the one of whom I said, 'The one coming after me ranks ahead of me, because he existed before me.' ") 16 Indeed, we have all received grace upon grace from his fullness, 17 for the law was given through Moses; grace and truth came through Jesus Christ. 18 No one has ever seen God. The one and only Son, who is himself God and is at the Father's side—he has revealed him.

That last paragraph makes it especially clear that God sent his Son, himself fully God, to take on flesh and reveal God to us. That Son, that Word, is Jesus Christ. Jesus is the fullest expression of everything God reveals to us in his written Word, the Bible. Jesus is the Word in the flesh.

The writer of Hebrews puts it this way:

Hebrews 1:1–3

**1** Long ago God spoke to the fathers by the prophets at different times and in different ways. 2 In these last days, he has spoken to us by his Son. God has appointed him heir of all things and made the universe through him. 3 The Son is the radiance of God's glory and the exact expression of his nature, sustaining all things by his powerful word. After making purification for sins, he sat down at the right hand of the Majesty on high.

We see here how Jesus is the culmination, the ultimate expression, of everything that can be humanly known about God. That is, because God is so far beyond us, we cannot know him as fully as he can know us. However, through Jesus, the Son who took on humanity, we can know God to the fullest of our human capacity. Jesus lacks nothing of God's (the Father's) glory, for Father, Son, and Spirit are one God. Everything we can perceive about God is perfectly and fully known through Jesus. This is why he told Philip, his disciple, "The one who has seen me has seen the Father" (Jn 14:9).

At the end of ch.1, I gave the analogy of getting a phone call from the love you were anxious to meet. This aural communication (representing the Holy Spirit) made the written communication (the Bible) come to life and make sense to you. This was the next best thing to a face-to-face meeting. I said the analogy falls short in that through the Holy Spirit God's *actual* presence is with you rather than just his voice. While there is no more intimate way to know God than through the Holy Spirit as he makes his Word come alive, there is still another aspect of this relationship that takes it to the full:

*Through Jesus we know God face-to-face.*

Now, I know that statement is not literal for us – not yet. The OT saints looked forward to the Christ. We look back at his first coming and wait excitedly for his return. As far as we can be sure, only people living in the first century saw him in the flesh. But we draw from that experience as we look forward to seeing him with our own eyes. Here is how the written Word and the Spirit make the Incarnate Word known to us here and now.

Be sure, we are not somehow missing out on a blessing because we didn't get to see Jesus in the first century. Thomas, one of Jesus' hand-picked Twelve, barely stumbled his way into real belief in Jesus, and he lived with him for three years! To him, Jesus proclaimed, "Because you have seen me, you have believed. Blessed are those who have not seen and yet believe" (Jn 20:29). That's us who live all these centuries later! We have a special blessing for believing in Jesus now in anticipation of seeing him. What's more, Jesus prayed for us, that we would be unified so that more would come to believe in him (17:20-21, more about that in the next section of this chapter).

Our spiritual eyes are opened to recognize Jesus much like the physical eyes of his disciples were opened on one occasion that is recorded in Luke 24. Jesus himself joined with them as they trekked the seven miles from Jerusalem to Emmaus. They were arguing about the situation following the crucifixion, and the reports that Jesus had raised from the dead. They were unable to recognize him, though he was right there walking with them (v.16). Jesus then proceeded to "[interpret] for them the things concerning himself in all the Scriptures." This is the same work he sent his Holy Spirit to do for us now. Then finally, as they sat down to a meal together their eyes were opened to recognize Jesus. They immediately shared their personal experiences with one another: "Weren't our hearts burning within us while he was talking with us on the road and explaining the Scriptures to us?"

If you have ever had the truth about Jesus proclaimed and explained from his Word, and then come to recognize Jesus through his Spirit, then I imagine you have had something similar happen. Didn't your heart burn within you?

If so, then *you have met Jesus.*

And if you have seen Jesus, you have seen the Father. That is, you have had the rare privilege to come to know God through his Spirit revealing his Son. His Son, Jesus, has made it possible for you to draw near to God by believing and trusting in his own perfection that purifies you through his own death and blood.

Jesus is the fully realized answer to the problem of sin. He is the perfect revelation of God to man, as he is fully man. He is the perfect solution to the problem of God's holiness, as he is fully God and perfectly holy. Now you can follow after him in his work of revealing himself to others, the work of a disciple.

**Talk it over**

*Why is it so important that God put on human skin and lived out a real human life in real history?*

*Why do you suppose God didn't offer this face-to-face incarnation experience for everyone in every time?*

*How was the disbelief of many who saw Jesus in the flesh just like the disbelief of many today?*

*How is your knowing Jesus today just as real and intimate as those who saw him in the flesh?*

**Pray and Worship**

Thank God for revealing himself perfectly through Jesus, for allowing us to know him through the Scriptures and through his Spirit.

Praise God for providing through Jesus the purification we need to safely draw near to him.

## Knowing God through His People

Here is where God's revelation comes full circle. God means to reveal himself in all the ways we've discussed. And he doesn't intend for it to stop with you. In his perfect grace and generosity, he wants to continue to expand his greatest gift – knowing him in all his glory – and share it with more and more people. In his perfect wisdom he has decided to let *you* participate in this most excellent endeavor.

The work of Jesus, the Son, in perfectly and fully revealing God, goes on. He now performs this work through his people. How does this process operate? I think a courtroom provides a helpful analogy.

If you have ever served as a juror, or if you've watched many courtroom scenes, whether real or fiction, you might know the responsibility handed to the jury. It is to consider the evidence in a matter and draw a conclusion that is "beyond a reasonable doubt." The court appointed lawyer's job is to present material evidence and witness testimony that supports the claim of his opening statement until the jury is convinced to that standard.

When considering the claims of Christianity, a non-believer is a juror. The material evidence presented comes through the means of general revelation (creation itself) and special revelation (the Bible) as we discussed in ch.1. God has presented evidence embedded in the nature of his creation, and in rational thought. He has offered his written Word as a document exhibit. Miraculous scenes are played out like video footage submitted for the jury's consideration. The circumstantial evidence is overwhelming, especially as presented by the most capable lead counsel – the Holy Spirit. The evidence is more than simply presented *before* the jury – it is like it is being presented *inside* of them! But there is one thing that pushes the case over the top – witnesses!

When someone is drawn to that point of belief that is beyond reasonable doubt, and they choose to both believe and follow Jesus, they change seats in this courtroom of Christian faith. They are no longer a juror but are now a witness. This is not to say a Christian has no doubts, just no reasonable ones. Whatever doubts remain give way to the mountain of incontrovertible evidence that has persuaded them to trust God. The doubts – though real – are swallowed up by what is sure.

The great privilege and desire for a Christ-follower to become a witness is a fundamental and governing reality for the disciple. John the Apostle, also called the Evangelist, expresses this idea in purpose statements for both his Gospel and one of his letters, 1 John.

John brilliantly constructs his Gospel as a theological work to pile up evidence that Jesus is the Eternal Son of God. He is God himself sent to finish the work of salvation. He sounds very much like our court advocate and states his purpose very clearly:

> John 20:30–31
>
> **30** Jesus performed many other signs in the presence of his disciples
> that are not written in this book. **31** But these are written so that you may
> believe that Jesus is the Messiah, the Son of God, and that by believing
> you may have life in his name.

John himself has come to belief and life through Jesus the Messiah, *and he wants others to have that same life* through coming to belief themselves. This desire is foundational in the prologue to 1 John:

> 1 John 1:1–4
>
> **1** What was from the beginning, what we have heard, what we have
> seen with our eyes, what we have observed and have touched with our
> hands, concerning the word of life—**2** that life was revealed, and we have
> seen it and we testify and declare to you the eternal life that was with the
> Father and was revealed to us—**3** what we have seen and heard we also
> declare to you, so that you may also have fellowship with us; and indeed

> our fellowship is with the Father and with his Son Jesus Christ. 4 We are
> writing these things so that our joy may be complete.

John here offers two related purpose statements: "that you may also have fellowship with us," and "that our joy may be complete." The second purpose is accomplished as a result of the first one, and its realization then comes to include the reader with those in the fellowship. The reader who believes is now part of both the "us" (v.3) and the "our" (v.4). John is saying that his joy as a disciple is incomplete until others are brought into fellowship with him and the other disciples, as their fellowship is with God.

The writer of Hebrews expressed the same desire present even back in the OT saints:

> Hebrews 11:30–40
>
> 30 By faith the walls of Jericho fell down after being marched around
> by the Israelites for seven days. 31 By faith Rahab the prostitute
> welcomed the spies in peace and didn't perish with those who disobeyed.
> 32 And what more can I say? Time is too short for me to tell about
> Gideon, Barak, Samson, Jephthah, David, Samuel, and the prophets,
> 33 who by faith conquered kingdoms, administered justice, obtained
> promises, shut the mouths of lions, 34 quenched the raging of fire,
> escaped the edge of the sword, gained strength in weakness, became
> mighty in battle, and put foreign armies to flight. 35 Women received
> their dead, raised to life again. Other people were tortured, not accepting
> release, so that they might gain a better resurrection. 36 Others
> experienced mockings and scourgings, as well as bonds and
> imprisonment. 37 They were stoned, they were sawed in two, they died by
> the sword, they wandered about in sheepskins, in goatskins, destitute,
> afflicted, and mistreated. 38 The world was not worthy of them. They
> wandered in deserts and on mountains, hiding in caves and holes in the
> ground.
> 39 All these were approved through their faith, but they did not receive
> what was promised, 40 since God had provided something better for us,
> so that they would not be made perfect without us.

Why did these saints fulfill such amazing accomplishments and endure such hardships?

"...so that they [OT saints] would not be made perfect without us [NT believers]." Those who went before us are lacking nothing in terms of justification by faith. The sense in which they are imperfect without us who come later is that God means for his community of faith to keep growing, filling up with more and more believers. Notice the calling that issues from this:

> Hebrews 12:1–2
>
> **12** Therefore, since we also have such a large cloud of witnesses
> surrounding us, let us lay aside every hindrance and the sin that so easily
> ensnares us. Let us run with endurance the race that lies before us,
> 2 keeping our eyes on Jesus, the source and perfecter of our faith. For the
> joy that lay before him, he endured the cross, despising the shame, and
> sat down at the right hand of the throne of God.

As his disciples, we follow after Jesus in the very same force that drove him: the joy of bringing others into the community of faith that celebrates his exaltation in heaven.

Jesus himself told his disciples that they would continue his work as his witnesses. And he would empower them for this work by giving them his Holy Spirit. They would in a sense continue to incarnate Jesus "in Jerusalem, in all Judea and Samaria, and to the end of the earth" (Acts 1:8).

Jesus intends to keep drawing new disciples to follow him. For this to happen, he will continue to reveal himself through his creation, his Word and his Spirit. The clincher is his own incarnation, his continued presence in the world through his Body, his Building, his House, his Church, his people. When someone is ready to consider the evidence, to consider the dangerous possibility of knowing God, he or she needs the compelling testimony of a witness. If you are a disciple of Jesus, they need to see him face-to-face through *you*!

**Talk it over**

*Given that the Apostle Paul describes the Christian life as "Christ in you," how does your face-to-face witness show the difference between knowing ABOUT Jesus versus KNOWING Jesus?*

*How is God's holiness important in our lives as witnesses?*

*According to the passages above, how should we Christians feel when our churches see few or no people coming to personally know Christ?*

*Do you think most Christians are being effective witnesses?*

**Pray and Worship**

Thank and praise the Lord for the witnesses that came before, like those in Hebrews 11 and the early Christians. And thank him for the witnesses that you have known personally, especially who have drawn you to Christ.

Ask the Lord to help you be faithful and effective as a witness, not missing opportunities or undermining them through unholy living or speech.

Thank the Lord for the privilege of following as a witness yourself, for participating in this expansion of joy.

# Part Two: Who Are Jesus' Disciples?

In Part One, I said that to become a disciple of Jesus, or to grow as his disciple, we must know him, cherish him, and must continue to grow in both knowing and cherishing him. This is because the disciple's goal is to be more and more like him. We examined how God reveals himself through his creation, his Word, his Spirit, his Incarnate Son Jesus, and through his people, which today are identified as the Church, the collection of Jesus' disciples.

In my introduction to Part One, I used an analogy of seeking employment at a company to illustrate the relationship between a worker and a CEO/owner as something like that between a disciple and the Lord Jesus. We want to join this company and work for this boss because he is awesome like no one else. In particular, he loves his employees so much he died for them.

In Part One, we were focused on this boss, Jesus, because he is the founder and head of the company, and the company exists for him. Every worker and every task are meant to make a big deal of him, and rightfully so. This is supremely true for Jesus for he is supremely awesome and deserving of all praise.

In Part Two, we will focus in on the employees, Jesus' disciples, for if we want to work for Jesus, we need to know what it means to be one of those disciples. We need to know and love and work with his other disciples. *How are they like everybody else, and how are they different?* To be and grow as disciples ourselves, we need to understand who we *are* and who we are *becoming. How do we become disciples that look more and more like Jesus?* We saw in ch.3 that we are Jesus' representatives now while we await his return, that we show the world what God is like. *How can we represent him well?*

# Ch.4 Like All Humans

First, we need to answer how Jesus' disciples are like every other human. For at least two important reasons, I want to assert that *apart from God's redemptive work through Jesus*, his disciples are no different from anyone else. That phrase in italics is what separates the truths of this chapter from those of the next. Apart from God's work, we who believe in and follow Jesus are no different from anyone else.

The first way this is true is that *everyone else is inherently no worse than Jesus' disciples*. That is, *all* of us humans bear the image of God. The second way is that *Jesus' disciples are inherently no better than everyone else*. That is, in their fallen state everyone *distorts* the image of God they bear. We'll explore each idea in turn.

## Made in God's Image (to Display His Glory)

My wife and I have been having fun watching our kids have kids. Each time one of our grandkids is born, one of the first topics of conversation is which parent they look like. They have mom's eyes, or dad's nose or hair. We make all our assessments, comment on how the cousins look alike, and on it goes. And then as the children grow older, not only does their "look" become better defined, but they start to develop mannerisms that also remind the onlooker of their parents.

We see this reality play out generation after generation, and it can be a source of great joy. We have little "Mini-me's" running around the planet! Of course, this can also be to our dismay when we see in our children the traits we don't so much like in ourselves. But the reality is no less true: our children are the spitting image of us.

The Bible uses language like this. Genesis 1:27 says God created mankind in his own image, or likeness. In a deliberate creative act, God made only mankind with this distinction. This is not said of the angels, nor of any animals, nor any other creature. What a special privilege!

And when the first man, Adam, began having children with Eve, his wife, this language is repeated: "Adam was 130 years old when he fathered a son *in his likeness, according to his image,* and named him Seth" (Gn 5:3, emphasis mine). Adam and Eve were the first parents who had the joyful experience of trying to figure out which features came from whom. Whatever those features looked like in Seth and their (many!) other children, the most obvious reality is that they were all humankind.

Every human being is inherently and by nature a creature that bears the image or likeness of God. The creature bears this image for the purpose of displaying the Creator's glory. This is a big deal! God so values human life that he reserves the harshest penalty for those who destroy it, and he does so precisely because we are made in his image (Gn 9:6). It was for this reason that God nearly destroyed all humanity from the earth, for men had become so violent and abusive toward other image-bearers that God's holy righteousness demanded justice.

But God is also perfectly gracious. To preserve his glory in his image-bearers, even in the face of the most widespread, egregious sin, God always spares a remnant of people for his own. He did so with Noah (Gn 6:7-8), he did so with Israel (Is 10-11; Rm 11:5), and he will do it at the end of this age when evil comes to a final climax (Rv 21:1-8).

Disciples of Jesus are today's expression of this remnant. Through Jesus Christ, God spares us and saves us to be his people who will bear his image forever. Together with OT saints and future disciples of Jesus we make up the Church. (This is what is meant when writing "Church" with a capital "C." When using a lower case "c" we are often referring primarily to the current, visible local communities of Jesus' disciples.)

*So, what makes disciples of Jesus different, that they are the ones spared?* We will look more in the next chapter at how Jesus-followers are different from everyone else, but for now the best brief answer to the question is to repeat it as a statement. What makes disciples of Jesus different *is* that they are the ones spared.

But we Christians are not spared because of our own natural merits. For every other human is also made in God's image and would in that sense deserve saving no less than we. In our natural state, we are all on the same plane. We all have inherent dignity as God's image-bearers. This is why we mourn the death of a human with ceremony and care. This is why we celebrate the birth of a new human life.

So, in what way do we bear God's image? It seems silly to say we look like God in a literal sense because God is spirit and transcends material forms (Jn 4:24). This is why God prohibited his people from fashioning physical images to worship, for those could only resemble his *creatures* and could not possibly represent *him* (Ex 20:4-5). God moved Moses to warn his people that Yahweh is beyond material form and that is why they only saw him manifested in smoke and fire on Mount Horeb (Dt 4:15). He understands our human hearts, that we would always tend to limit God by fashioning him into images of his creation (vv.16-19). God appeared without a definite form to remind us he is Spirit, far beyond what we his creatures can know. Bearing his image does not mean that we can display *all* that God is. It does mean he has chosen *something* of who he is to display in every human.

How, then, are we in God's likeness? Many would suggest that our own spirituality – our unique ability to relate to God – sets us apart from all other earthly creatures, and this certainly is true. Others focus on the mandate to rule that God gave man in Genesis 1:28 as the primary distinctive of God's image in us. Just after we are told that we are image-bearers came the command, "Be fruitful, multiply, fill the earth, and subdue it. Rule the fish of the sea, the birds of the sky, and every creature that crawls on the earth." It certainly makes sense that we reflect God's glory in ruling well over his earthly creation.

The discussion about what traits make up the image of God in man draws plenty of attention and a variety of suggestions beyond these, but it seems reasonable to conclude that *any* way we can properly reflect God's glory and majesty is an expression of his image in us. The point is that *every* human bears this image. It is bound up in human nature. So then, those who follow Jesus as his disciples bear in themselves the image of God.

**Talk it over**

Read Gn 1:27 and 2:19-24...

> 27 So God created man in his own image;
> he created him in the image of God;
> he created them male and female.

> 19 The LORD God formed out of the ground every wild animal and
> every bird of the sky, and brought each to the man to see what he
> would call it. And whatever the man called a living creature, that
> was its name. 20 The man gave names to all the livestock, to the birds

of the sky, and to every wild animal; but for the man no helper was
found corresponding to him. 21 So the LORD God caused a deep sleep
to come over the man, and he slept. God took one of his ribs and
closed the flesh at that place. 22 Then the LORD God made the rib he
had taken from the man into a woman and brought her to the man.
23 And the man said:

> This one, at last, is bone of my bone
> and flesh of my flesh;
> this one will be called "woman,"
> for she was taken from man.

24 This is why a man leaves his father and mother and bonds
with his wife, and they become one flesh.

After the creation of everything in six days recorded in Genesis 1, the narrative backs up and zooms in with more detail on the creation of humankind in ch.2.

*How does this special focus on the creation of humankind indicate the special place God gave us in his creation?*

*Why is it significant that the image of God is expressed in both male and female?*

*Why is God justified in prohibiting worship of images rather than only himself?*

*What are some ways you have seen humans violate the image of God in others?*

*What are some ways you have seen God's image shine in others, maybe even been surprised by it?*

## Distortions of God's Image

Disciples of Jesus, like all other humans, possess inherent dignity as creatures who bear the image of God who created them. That dignity and glory is still evident today, though you may have to look pretty hard to see it. *Why is God's good image so hard to see in humanity?* Well, the reason is because we all share the same problem: *sin.*

Sin is the reason that God once destroyed all humankind but eight souls (Gn 7:11-23). Sin distorts and mutes the image of God in us, sometimes so much that it may be hard to see at all. What kind of language do we use to describe the most monstrous people, like Hitler, Bin Laden or Ted Bundy? We call them animals or beasts (Rm 1:21-23; 28-32). What we are expressing is the overwhelming way in which their sin has all but swallowed up our ability to see God's image in them.

But sin warps us all. It may seem less evident in you or me than in Hitler, but it is no less true. And it is no less true for any Christian, in terms of his or her natural state. The expression of God's image is distorted in all of us.

We talked in ch.2 about how our sin disqualifies us from fellowship with God, turning a situation meant for our greatest joy into a death sentence. In the same way, our sin also corrupts our great privilege as image-bearers. We were created to display God's glory among humankind and before all others of God's creatures, but our sin distorts that glory and ruins God's reputation.

Think back to the lunchroom scene and the table that seemed out of our league. This table is where Jesus is. He is (for the sake of analogy) the coolest kid in the school – the coolest kid in *any* school. He started the Jesus Club. The club's one purpose is that we could hang out with him and make a big deal of him – the most fun thing possible! So, at his table we talk about how great he is, we dress like him and act like him. Just like we might excitedly recall an amazing game-winning buzzer-beater by a star athlete, we reenact all the cool things Jesus does. And then he gives us one duty – go get more club members by bragging on Jesus while we look like him, talk like him and dress like him.

Of course, this is all inappropriately narcissistic for anybody but Jesus. But in his case, hanging out with him *is* the greatest joy. He is the God who created us for that (Col 1:15-16). And he created us in his image to represent him and to bring others to hang out with him. But that's not what happened. Not with the first people he placed in paradise, and not with any of us since.

Instead of bragging on him, we make *ourselves* the center of attention. We try to change the name of the club, or at least pick someone else to be Jesus, and we declare ourselves the president of the club. We don't very much look like Jesus or talk like him or act like him. Eventually, Jesus is nowhere to be found because we have hijacked his club and made it our own.

This is the problem for all humans. We misrepresent God, and that is the worst possible offence against the One in whom all reality exists, the One who literally holds us together (Col 1:17). If at any moment God ceased to sustain our existence – poof! – we would not exist. Yet somehow, we think little of him. His own glory with which he endowed us we twist and distort and misrepresent.

This does not change that we *are* image-bearers, but it completely reverses and destroys the *effect* of bearing his image. We were created to show God as trustworthy and kind, but in how we live we make him seem deceitful or mean. He is perfectly just and righteous, but when we mistreat people to serve our own interests, we make him seem self-serving. In all the ways we do not live up to our purpose as image-bearers, we cause God to bear all our sinful traits, for he has chosen to attach his reputation to ours. And as bad as it is for *any* human to misrepresent God, it is even *worse* to do so while calling yourself a *Christian*.

But it happens. All the time. We are all – Christians included – distorted expressions of God's image. I am by nature no more human, and no more an image-bearer, than Hitler. This is what I meant by the statement that *Jesus' disciples are inherently no better than everyone else*. The potential disciple and the committed disciple alike need to understand and remember this truth. It keeps us focused on the *only* thing that makes the distinction between Christians and non-Christians – God's work of restoration.

That work finds its crux in the statement above, that *we cause God to bear all our sinful traits*. In terms of our rebellion, this is something *we* cause. In terms of the eternal solution, it is something *God* caused. He planned it before the foundation of the world, and it is the reason he sent the Son to take on human flesh (Eph 1:3-8; 1 Pt 1:18-20). Jesus came to bear all our sin, all the ways we have and can and would ever distort and fall short of the full and proper expression of the image of God. He felt all the shame of the ruined reputation of God as though he himself were responsible. And he paid the full extent of the penalty for all of it through his death. He who is the *true* and *exact* image of God (Php 2:6; Heb 1:3) restored God's reputation in his own resurrected and eternal life. Now he repairs the warping of the image in those who follow him, those who put sin to death and live in his eternal life. How he carries out this restoration will be the subject of the next chapter.

**Talk it over**

*How did you feel as you read through the Jesus Club analogy above? Why does it feel so wrong for anyone – even Jesus – to draw that kind of attention to himself?*

*How does your natural reaction to the scenario reveal how truly wrong it is for us to rob the glory that only Jesus deserves?*

Read Ps 14:1-3...

> 1 The fool says in his heart, "There's no God."
> They are corrupt; they do vile deeds.
> There is no one who does good.
> 2 The LORD looks down from heaven on the human race,
> to see if there is one who is wise,
> one who seeks God.
> 3 All have turned away;
> all alike have become corrupt.
> There is no one who does good,
> not even one.

These words are repeated in Ps 53:1-3, and they are quoted by Paul in Rm 3:9-12...

> 9 What then? Are we any better off? Not at all! For we have
> already charged that both Jews and Gentiles are all under sin, 10 as
> it is written:

**There is no one righteous, not even one.**
**11 There is no one who understands;**
**there is no one who seeks God.**
**12 All have turned away;**
**all alike have become worthless.**
**There is no one who does what is good,**
**not even one.**

Then Paul summarizes in v.23: "...all have sinned and fall short of the glory of God."

*According to these passages, how pervasive is the problem of sin in humanity – whom does it affect?*

*Why is it important to realize that the image of God looks distorted even in Jesus' disciples?*

*Why is it even worse for someone calling himself or herself a Christian to misrepresent God?*

**Pray and Worship**

Confess to God that (even as a Christian) you fall short of representing his glory.

Thank the Lord Jesus for bearing the bad reputation you caused by your sin, and for paying for sin's penalty in his death. Praise him for his own power of resurrection life, and that he gives you that power.

Ask Christ to continue to restore his image in you, and to help you submit to and cooperate with his work.

# Ch.5 Called Out: Being Restored to God's Image in Christ

I said in ch.3 that Jesus is the culmination, the ultimate expression, of everything that can be humanly known about God. As the Eternal Son who is the exact expression of God's nature (Heb 1:3), Jesus possesses the nature of deity that infinitely transcends what is knowable in his human nature. So, he is *more* than the perfect human, more than we can ever be as image-bearers. Still, Jesus in his humanity is the ultimate image-bearer who displays God's image to the maximum human extent. As such, he is the perfect picture of what we are called to be ourselves. We cannot attain to all that the Son is, but we *are* called to be everything we were meant to be as image-bearers. And Jesus the Son shows us fully that potential. In the last chapter we came to understand that our sin causes us to fall short of the full glory of the image we bear. The miracle of union with Christ is that we can not only see in him our full potential, but we can grow toward it.

## Standing and Growing: Justification and Sanctification

It is important to understand that there are two temporal aspects of Christian growth. That is, part of God's work in the disciple is a *de facto* reality upon conversion but another part is ongoing. The moment one believes and trusts Christ alone for forgiveness, for payment of sin and for eternal life, that person is *justified* before God. That is a gift. We do not help Jesus justify us. It is completely his work. Any natural response – thanksgiving, praise, doing things that please God – are *effects* of this justification but they do not in any sense *cause* it. God sees us together with Christ, and so sees us as righteous and perfect in his own righteousness and perfection. We use the term *standing* to describe this: We have a right standing with God. This means what is true of Jesus is declared to be true about us. This is *already* the case, even when we have not performed one obedient and faithful act except to believe! This is why a criminal who was crucified and dying next to Jesus could plead for mercy, offer nothing but belief and could be reassured, "Today you will be with me in paradise" (Lk 23:40-3). When we believe, God accepts us as righteous like his Son.

But every Christian, even (especially!) after many years of faith, will confess that they are still in reality far short of Jesus' perfection. We never in this life reach the end of our growing process. How can God act as though this work of restoration is already complete?

God can speak this way because of his sovereign power. Whatever he has decreed he will do is certain. The Apostle Paul expresses this certainty in Philippians 1:6: "I am sure of this, that he who started a good work in you will carry it on to completion until the day of Christ Jesus." To the Ephesians, Paul clearly states that "God chose us in [Christ], before the foundation of the world, to be holy and blameless in love before him." He uses the present tense to say, "In [Christ] we have redemption through his blood, the forgiveness of our trespasses, according to the riches of his grace." Paul then writes of the ongoing activity of God, "who works out everything in agreement with the purpose of his will, so that we ... might bring praise to his glory."

### Restored through Union with Christ (Justification)

In writing to the Galatians, Paul carefully sifts justification out of the greater process of salvation. He makes it very clear that nothing we do can help justify us before God. In Gal 3:6 he states that it is only by believing God that we are "credited...for righteousness." Our justification – our righteous *standing* – is a gift. This does not mean that obedient living – our righteous *works* – are not a part of salvation. They are.

My point here is to make clear that the remaining content of this chapter is about becoming more like Jesus, but it is *not* about anything that makes the Christian more acceptable to God. He accepts us because of Christ through our faith. Since Christ is perfect, our standing is sure. What *is* accomplished in our ongoing renovation – what is usually called *sanctification* – is that God makes us more and more like the reality he already created and fully accepts in us through Christ.

Think back to our lunchroom illustration and the Jesus Club. Imagine Jesus, who started and presides over and is the object of the club, wears the coolest jacket imaginable. To use an old term, this jacket is *righteous!* When Jesus hosts meetings at his Father's house, nobody is admitted unless they wear the righteous jacket. So, upon joining the club Jesus gives everyone his jacket in their own size. Even the newest member of the club has a righteous jacket from day one. That's justification.

Now, because the members worship Jesus, over time they don't just wear the Jesus jacket, but they also start *acting* like Jesus. They pick up his mannerisms and his speech and they do whatever he wants. That's sanctification. The more they hang out with Jesus, the more they act like him.

Jesus' Father sees everyone with Jesus jackets as righteous. They are accepted at the house already. But the Father will make sure that over time everyone who gets his Son's jacket becomes more and more like his Son. Eventually, the whole club will be called to the house permanently, and then everyone will be like Jesus completely and permanently – we call that *glorification!* That happens in the life to come. For now, we are focused on the rest of *this* life, when God is transforming us in preparation for that eternal state.

Justification is totally God's work, a gift to be received by faith. From our perspective, this triggers the ongoing work of sanctification. This too is God's work, but we actively participate in it. That is why Paul calls the Philippians to "work out [their] own salvation with fear and trembling" (Phi 2:12)." Paul is not talking about justification here but rather about the ongoing work of expressing holiness and obedience. Still, we would neither desire nor carry out these works apart from God working in us (v.13). That means God receives *all* the glory for *all* aspects of salvation in *all* of us. He gives his disciples a righteous standing in Christ. Then he transforms us into the image of Christ himself.

How does he do that? He transforms us through his own Presence, through his Word, and through his community, the church. We will look at three aspects of this restoration work: He changes what his disciples believe, what they want and what they do.

**Talk it over**

Talk about a healthy parent-child relationship:

*When the child is a newborn baby, what is the basis for the parent's love?*

*As the child gets older, what kinds of expectations does the parent have for the child to progress?*

*No matter how well the child does or doesn't meet expectations, should the basis for the parent's love ever change?*

*Does God expect you to grow and mature spiritually? Does his love for you depend on your spiritual progress?*

## Restored through His Transforming Presence, Word, and Community (Sanctification)

When we are united with Christ by faith, we are then filled with his presence through the Holy Spirit. Christ himself lives within us. This reality itself is transforming. God gave us a powerful example of how his presence transforms us way back in Exodus. Moses, the man God hand-picked to lead his people out of Egyptian bondage, experienced it first-hand. You might call his transformation an "afterglow." Some of us Christians used to hang out after a church gathering and called that an afterglow, but Moses experienced something more dramatic than we did.

Remember the scene from Exodus 19 that I mentioned in ch.2? The glory of the Lord boomed and flashed in a crazy thunderstorm on top of Mount Sinai as Moses went up to receive the Ten Commandments. It was said later of Moses that "the LORD would speak to [him] face to face, just as a man speaks with his friend" (33:11; see also Nu 12:8). But these were no mere *mano a mano* conversations. They were transformational to Moses. He wanted so much to know the Lord in his glory that he requested to see it (v.18). The Lord did not grant his full request because – as we discussed earlier – for Moses in his natural state it would have been fatal (v.20). Still, God did grant a special encounter with a manifestation of his glory which he knew Moses could survive (vv.21-23).

As Moses descended from Sinai his face literally glowed "as a result of his speaking with the LORD" (34:29). In fact, this seems to have continued as a pattern when Moses would speak with the LORD and then come out to pass the messages on to the people. He would put a veil over his face because it was so bright that it freaked them out (vv.30-35)!

The NT is quite clear that it is normal for something similar to happen with Christians. Perhaps our faces are not filled with blinding light, but we *are* transformed by the ongoing presence of the Living God in us. It does mean *something* that we are the light of the world, and that we are to shine before others (Mt 5:14-16). A true disciple of Christ will noticeably stick out in a dark world. And the most foundational reason is that we live in the presence of Christ's Spirit. Christ is transforming us by living in us (Mt 28:20b; Rm 8:11; Col 1:27).

Parents all understand the simple truth as it affects their kids: we start to act like those with whom we spend a lot of time. That's why good parents have strong opinions and directives about who they let their children hang around. This is why the Christian exercises spiritual disciplines we will mention in Part III, to conscientiously be focused and aware of the transforming presence of Christ through his Spirit. As Paul puts it, "We all, with unveiled faces, are looking as in a mirror at the glory of the Lord and are being transformed into the same image from glory to glory; this is from the Lord who is the Spirit." (2 Cor 3:18) Our direct encounter with the Lord transforms us from our fallen version of his image to become more and more like the perfect version expressed in Jesus.

So, Christ's Spirit gives us the internal power for transformation. And as we learned in ch.1, his Spirit uses the tool of Scripture. The Spirit uses the Word of God not only to show us himself but also to transform us into what we see. The crucial place the Bible holds in this transformational process is especially clear in the NT. It is effective in transformation because it is supernatural (1 Th 2:13) and it is surgical in its precision (Heb 4:12). The psalmist proclaimed that the word of God is *life* (Ps 119:25,107), and Jesus said the same thing (Mt 4:4; Jn 6:63). How does the Spirit use Scripture to transform us?

First, he transforms what we *believe*. He targets the mind to bring wrong thinking around to right thinking. This is especially clear in Rm 12:2 and Eph 4:20-24:

Romans 12:2

[2] Do not be conformed to this age, but be transformed by the renewing of your mind, so that you may discern what is the good, pleasing, and perfect will of God.

Ephesians 4:20–24

[20] But that is not how you came to know Christ, [21] assuming you heard
about him and were taught by him, as the truth is in Jesus, [22] to take off
your former way of life, the old self that is corrupted by deceitful desires,
[23] to be renewed in the spirit of your minds, [24] and to put on the new self,
the one created according to God's likeness in righteousness and purity
of the truth.

The transformation of the mind does not only bring us around to believe *rightly* but it also brings us to believe more *deeply*. In John's Gospel belief in Jesus is a common theme, and John used it across a wide spectrum. Some who "believed in Jesus" had such a tenuous and fickle belief that they walked away when Jesus taught things that were difficult to follow (Jn 2:23; 6:26-29,60-66). Even the Twelve struggled with their belief, but – with the exception of Judas – they were convinced enough to hang in with Jesus (vv.66-70). Their belief entered a totally new zip code when they witnessed the empty tomb and a resurrected Lord (20:3-10; 24-29)!

Jesus continues to do the same thing today with our belief. His Spirit reveals him to us, giving us "Aha!" moments when we read the Bible, hear it faithfully taught, when we worship together, when we fellowship around the gospel, and sometimes in the most unlikely circumstances of life. Every time we get a fresh glimpse of Jesus' glory, we are drawn farther in our transformation to be like him.

It is important to realize that the gospel itself is the core of all transforming belief. That is, whatever truth is represented in each "Aha!" moment, it could rightly be said that we are more accurately and or more deeply believing the gospel. This is why Christians are commanded to gather regularly, so that we might continually help one another believe the gospel more fully. We'll talk more about that too in Part III.

So, Jesus gives us his Spirit presence, the Bible itself, and the Bible-centered community of other Christians to transform us through what we believe. As this happens, he also transforms what we *desire*. This, too, is a gospel reality. The gospel message draws us to see Christ as the ultimate object of affection and adoration. Without the gospel we are dulled in our spiritual senses and begin to crave or seek satisfaction in lesser things. The gospel draws our hearts to worship God alone, draws us to Jesus who saves us, who is our life. Jesus is the only source for satisfaction. We already discussed that the *Father* is satisfied with us through Jesus. But it is also true that only at the feet of Jesus do *we* find satisfaction for our souls.

Finding true and ultimate satisfaction in Jesus is the essence of what we mean when we talk about worship. In worship we declare worth, and true worship the way the Bible defines it belongs only to the true God. He is more than *most* deserving of worship – he is *alone* deserving of it. This is why Jesus told the parables about treasure in Matthew 13:44-46. Jesus describes the kingdom of heaven as worth giving up everything in this life. But the treasure of the heavenly kingdom is its King... Jesus. This is made clear when Paul talks of the "surpassing value of knowing Christ Jesus [his] Lord" (Phi 3:7-9). For Christ, Paul had "suffered the loss of all things and considered them as dung, so that [he] may gain Christ and be found in him..." Paul told the Ephesians that God the Father "has blessed us with *every* spiritual blessing in the heavens *in Christ*" (Eph 1:3, emphasis mine). Two chapters later he describes his mission as one "to proclaim to the Gentiles the incalculable riches in Christ" (3:8).

That Jesus should be prized this way – a disciple's top priority – was the reason that Jesus himself said, "The one who loves a father or a mother more than me is not worthy of me; the one who loves a son or daughter more than me is not worthy of me" (Mt 10:37). Jesus was not saying we should not love our family members or anyone else. Rather, he was saying that our love for him should exceed any other love, even to the point that if a family member rejects us, we will continue to love Christ. In fact, we will never love anyone else as we ought *unless* we love Jesus above all else.

Discovering Christ's ultimate worth – and deepening in one's awareness of it – is how we are transformed by the gospel. Initially, we see Christ as our one great *need*. But more and more over time we come to know Christ as our one great *desire*. This transforms us into true worshipers, not just for

90 minutes on a Sunday but throughout every day as we come to value Jesus more than anything or anyone else.

And as our beliefs and our desires are transformed, then gradually but surely our actions and behavioral patterns are transformed. We become more and more obedient to Christ's commands, acting more and more like the one we are coming to know and worship. Old sinful habits give way to new godly ones, such that – to one degree or another – should an old friend run into us today, they may well ask, "What happened to *you*?!"

That is exactly why God does this transforming work. It shows off his greatness and his great work to others, so they may come to know him and be transformed too. This is what Paul is writing about in Ephesians 2:1-10:

> And you were dead in your trespasses and sins 2 in which you previously lived according to the ways of this world, according to the ruler of the power of the air, the spirit now working in the disobedient. 3 We too all previously lived among them in our fleshly desires, carrying out the inclinations of our flesh and thoughts, and we were by nature children under wrath as the others were also. 4 But God, who is rich in mercy, because of his great love that he had for us, 5 made us alive with Christ even though we were dead in trespasses. You are saved by grace! 6 He also raised us up with him and seated us with him in the heavens in Christ Jesus, 7 so that in the coming ages he might display the immeasurable riches of his grace through his kindness to us in Christ Jesus. 8 For you are saved by grace through faith, and this is not from yourselves; it is God's gift—9 not from works, so that no one can boast. 10 For we are his workmanship, created in Christ Jesus for good works, which God prepared ahead of time for us to do.

God prepared before we even existed that he would restore his image in us through Christ Jesus so that he might display the immeasurable riches of his grace, not only in this life but the next, and not only before other people but before the heavenly creatures too!

This is who Jesus' disciples are. We are broken humans just like any other. But we are also those that God has chosen to know – and be known by – his Son, so that he would show his greatness to the universe by transforming our lives.

**Talk it over**

Describe the version of you that people knew years ago. *How are you different today? How might old friends who haven't seen you for years react to the way you are now?*

*What kind of expectation is normal for a Christian, based on what Paul said in Eph 2:10?*

*What are areas where you still struggle the most with worshiping and obeying Jesus?*

*How does the reality of the justification you already have help you with these frustrations with your own journey of sanctification?*

**Pray and Worship**

Thank God that even on your worst day you are justified through faith in Christ. Thank him that you are accepted and perfectly and completely loved.

Ask God to give you a growing and deepening desire for Christ, to value and worship him alone, to choose obedience and holiness over anything less.

# Part Three: What Do Jesus' Disciples Do?

In Part One, I drew from the workplace analogy to focus on God as a kind of ultimate boss. He is ultimate goodness and power and love, a boss so awesome that his "employees" don't just work for him they *worship* him. As the definition of perfect goodness, he offers us the best possible gift – the privilege of intimately knowing him and participating in his amazing creative and redemptive work. He has revealed himself to us in his "workplace" of the world in which we live, and he has given us a special revelation – an "employee handbook" – called the Bible. Further, he has given us his own Spirit – a sort of "executive assistant" – sent to help us decode spiritual realities to which we have been blinded by our fallen, sinful nature. We also saw how God sent his eternal Son, Jesus, to make his written Word come to life in flesh and blood before us in the Incarnate Word. Remember, God's infinite perfection goes far beyond what we can know as mere humans, but we have access to everything that *can* be humanly known about God through his Word, his Son and his Spirit. We who live long after Jesus walked the earth in the flesh know him by faith, looking forward to when we – like his first disciples – will see him face to face (1 Cor 13:12; 1 Jn 3:2). The last important way that God reveals himself, and reveals Jesus his Son, is through those who follow Jesus. Together, the group of individual Christ-followers (Christians) make up the Body of Christ, and we continue to display our "boss" and his work to others until the end of this age.

In Part Two, I focused on this "workforce" who both worship and represent the "boss." We explored how these people are just like every other human in two key ways. First, we are all made in God's image or likeness for the purpose of expressing his glory. Second, we are all fallen, and because of our rebellion – our sin – we have all come to distort that glorious image of God. Then we talked about how disciples of Jesus become different from everyone else. This is God's work, not an inherent trait in us but rather his work with which we willingly cooperate. (And we have God to thank for even this cooperative attitude, see Php 2:13). Through Christ he is restoring those who respond in faith to his call to himself. God sees us as righteous with and through his perfectly righteous Son, Jesus. We continue to draw close to him through this access Jesus provides. God's renovation comes through Jesus' own transforming presence through his Spirit, through the Bible and through the community of disciples, the Church.

So, in Part One we learned about the "boss," Jesus. In Part Two we learned about his "employees," Jesus' disciples. Now, in Part Three I will discuss the *activities* of those disciples: *What do Jesus' disciples do?* Or, in a practical sense, I will respond to the question a new Christ-follower would ask: *What do I do now?* I have said that during this time when Jesus is physically away from us that he continues to make himself known through his Body, the church. Now we will look more specifically at how this happens.

In a workplace there are job descriptions and standard operating procedures, and emergency plans and so on. And there are meetings. We will see much the same with the church. The NT shows us not only what Christians are to *believe* but also what they are to *do*. We will explore three main arenas of activity. First, I will talk about what disciples of Jesus do as they *scatter*, as they live in their own circles of influence in the world among both Christians and non-Christians. Second, I will discuss what disciples do when they *gather* together in meetings with other Christians. Then I will briefly consider the space in between scattering and gathering, the moments when the disciple privately pursues a deeper relationship with God. It might seem counter-intuitive to take these arenas in that order. The new worker might ask, "*But don't I need training before I go out on the job?*" My hope is to undermine any tendency to think that a disciple must wait for some perceived benchmark of Christian maturity before he or she is ready to represent Jesus in the world. The fact is that we become ambassadors for Jesus as soon as we have believed and trusted him ourselves. While it is true that we naturally grow in our ability to express our faith in word and deed, and we should also diligently *train* to do so, we already have the basic tools we need to share our faith from our earliest moments as Christ-followers.

A brilliant case in point is found in John's Gospel, ch.4. In that text Jesus engaged a woman in a conversation where he revealed his identity as the Messiah. She was so impressed with his understanding of her life and his offer of living water that she believed in him. What did she immediately do? She went back to the people of her town and told them about how amazing Jesus was, that he might just be the Messiah (v.28). Before long, many from her town also believed in Jesus. First, they were persuaded by the woman's testimony about Jesus, but then they came to know him personally (v.42).

This is a picture of the privilege and opportunity before every disciple, even immediately following their own conversion to faith.

So, in the first chapter of Part Three we will walk through three interwoven ways we disciples do what this woman did, how we testify about Jesus before others. We do so by proclaiming the *biblical message of the gospel*, by proclaiming our *personal encounter with Jesus* (usually called our testimony) and by backing up our proclamation with *holy living* that shows a transformed life. This section deals generally with what we call *evangelism*.

Then, in the next two chapters of Part Three I will list the key ways that disciples grow in their faith so that they better understand and proclaim the message, they continue to deepen in their relationship with Jesus and they become more disciplined in holy living that shows the world what he is like. In other words, we come together to grow in Christ so that we may be better *evangelists*. This growth happens through what we call *spiritual disciplines*. These activities are expressed both corporately and individually. We will first concentrate on the corporate arena, on the things disciples do when they come together for growth (ch.7). Then in ch.8 we will touch briefly on how spiritual disciplines find expression in private times of devotion for individual disciples. Both arenas are critical for the Christian as each stimulates the other.

Once we see how disciples proclaim the gospel even as they continue to deepen in their own faith, we will pause to prepare for a sobering reality that has faced every disciple since those first ones hand-picked by Jesus himself. Many people are not impressed with Jesus as we are. They do not worship him as he deserves. Many of these are not bothered by your faith and are even willing to listen as you relate the gospel to them. But many do not want to hear it, and are very bothered by your message, your lifestyle and even your presence. Some of those will cause trouble for you. In ch.9, we'll consider the question, *"How does the disciple handle a hostile world?"*

Then in ch.10 I will summarize the *goal* of all the disciple's activities, and in fact, the goal of this entire resource. It is that the process comes full circle and continues to repeat itself, that disciples make other disciples that make other disciples, and so on. This has been the plan, the command and work of Jesus since he began his Church in the first century. The ongoing realization of that goal lends itself to the ultimate goal of all of God's redemptive work – that he is given all glory, as he alone deserves.

**Talk it over**
Read back through Jn 4:1-42

*What about this brief encounter with Jesus do you suppose gave this woman the boldness to tell others about him?*

*What kinds of things may tend to keep you from telling others about Jesus?*

*To what was Jesus referring in v.34 when he spoke of his "food" and "his work"? What "harvest" was Jesus "reaping" (vv.35-36)?*

*What does this story tell us about the importance and urgency of proclaiming Jesus to others?*

**Pray and Worship**
Think of any disciples through whom God worked to proclaim Jesus to you, and then praise God for his kind and generous work in and through them on your behalf.
Ask God to give you boldness to proclaim Christ to others, and to help you see and seize every opportunity in every way to do so.

# Ch.6 Proclaiming the Gospel as They Scatter (Evangelism)

## Proclamation through the Biblical Message

Picture an ancient kingdom, and walled city with a watchman atop the wall above the gate. He sees a tiny cloud of dust begin to rise up from the dry ground far outside the city. Over a period of minutes, the cloud grows, and the watchman can see a figure coming into view. Someone is running urgently toward him. By now, he is approaching the outer rings of agriculture and the scattered farmers and workers who are laboring for produce. The runner seems to be going from pocket to pocket, delivering some quick message to everyone he encounters as he approaches the city. When he finally reaches the wall, the watchman learns what all this is about. The runner is a herald. He has been sent by a foreign king with this message: Come be a part of my kingdom, for this kingdom will be destroyed, and only those who trust in the protection I provide through my own son, the king and heir, will survive.

Now, this herald has a simple message. There are certainly many deeper things to know about this king and his kingdom, and the more the herald knows, the better he can speak on the king's behalf. But urgency has sent him out, and the herald understands what he must to get the basic idea across. He knows the king is most powerful. He knows the king is most benevolent. He knows the king is generous to send him with a message of rescue before sure destruction.

Disciples of Jesus are heralds. We are more but not less. The first and most basic activity of a disciple is to share with others the message that has brought salvation and life to themselves. The Bible uses the term "gospel" to refer to this message. The term means "good news." At first, you might wonder how it is good news that one's kingdom is going to be destroyed. Well, the gospel – when it is complete and true – has bad news built in on the front end. Without the built-in bad news, the good news is not only less compelling, it is misleading.

All kinds of comic (as opposed to tragic) literature easily illustrate the first reality. We realize that good stories – whether told orally, read in books or acted out on stage or in a movie – all have plot arcs. The tension created by some kind of conflict elevates the relief and elation that comes with the resolution of the plot line when the protagonist prevails.

Every Hallmark Channel "chick flick" follows this pattern. Characters and plot lines are set up. The characters that clearly belong together are being drawn together through circumstances. Then eventually some kind of trouble comes, whether an actual betrayal or a misunderstanding where one is perceived. *Will they see the truth? Will they reconcile before it is too late?* No matter how cheesy the presentation, no matter how predictable the outcome, when I watch these shows with my wife, I still notice that I feel the tension and release.

The real-life story of every human being follows this arc. In fact, we Christians commonly refer to the "gospel arc" or "biblical arc of God's redemptive work." The arc begins with God's creation – things were perfect (Gn 1-2). Then conflict was introduced by the serpent's deception and man's sin (Gn 3). Hope was introduced by God's declaration that he would provide a rescue (v.15) and that hope begins taking shape with a promise to Abraham (Gn 12:1-3), which will be fulfilled by God's Servant (Is 9:6-7; ch.53). *When will this turmoil end? When will humanity's Rescuer come?* Then Jesus shows up. Finally, we think, resolution will come. He's the one! But the plot thickens. Those who should have best understood who Jesus was, and why he came, rejected him, and they murdered him! The plot arc bottoms out for two days while Jesus' body lies in a tomb, and those first disciples mourn in despair. Peter had rightly proclaimed (Jn 6:68), "To whom (else) will we go? You have the words of eternal life." Now the Holy One of God was dead.

Then on the third day, the moment for which all of human history had been waiting came! Jesus rose from the dead, and his message and identity were vindicated before all the world by the empty tomb! (If you need to pause for a moment because a shout or clap or a celebration dance is bubbling out of you, go ahead!) He showed himself to his disciples and set them on fire to begin a movement that is still growing today. He left to prepare a place for us, and he sent us his Spirit to empower and direct us until he returns and establishes his kingdom fully and visibly forever.

But not all tension is resolved. The already/not yet status of his kingdom and our salvation compels us forward. Like a die-hard fan of a movie series, we wait for the sequel. And there are millions who have not yet even heard this story, let alone trusted in the King. That is where YOU come in. And me. And all who are disciples of Jesus.

We tell this story every chance we get. We have a head start, for the Bible teaches that everyone is innately aware of the basic plotline, at least the parts about God's creating and about our failure to measure up or to save ourselves. Many need the details filled in, but they have a sense of their need. They have already disappointed themselves over and over, failing to live up to their *own* standards. It is not much of a stretch to think they have failed Someone's even *higher* standards. And that prepares them to hope for a Savior. Who wouldn't prefer a comedy to a tragedy, a happy ending over a bummer?

And then they are right in front of you. You have the information that determines the outcome for them – comedy or tragedy? *Will you speak up? What should you say?*

Jesus has told his disciples - that's you – to proclaim the good news. Put the words to the story they already sense is there. Name the God who created them. Show them the Deceiver who duped them. Help them understand their rebel hearts, and the problem their sin creates before a holy God. Then give them the plot twist they were hoping for: a hero who sacrificed everything to bring a happy ending. Introduce them to Jesus.

This is what disciples do. We proclaim the biblical message to the outsider.

Now, depending on the conversation and your own personal growth in biblical knowledge you may share very few details or a lot of them. You likely won't often share a Bible reference (like "John 3:16"), and many times probably will not actually recite Scripture. Generally, what is most helpful is that you are telling in your own words what the Bible has said. If they are willing to sit down and read the Bible along with you, that is a great opportunity – take it! However, many people are at least initially reluctant to do that even though they may be quite willing to listen while you share what the Bible says conversationally.

What is especially important is that you are sharing what the Bible communicates (even in your own words) rather than offering someone your own opinions or philosophy. It is what *God* communicated that delivers the power to rescue someone from tragedy. You are the *messenger*, but you do not come up with your own message. A herald doesn't do that. That should give you both encouragement and caution. When you proclaim the truth to someone, the message does not depend on you – it is powerful on its own when you deliver it. But you must deliver it faithfully, not corrupt it by wandering off into your own speculations or diluting it because you don't want to offend.

You have heard and believed the words of life. Those words are what you must proclaim. This means saying what the Bible says. More specifically, and more concisely, what you must share is the *gospel*. Think of the gospel as the CliffsNotes of the great drama of redemption that is laid out by the whole Bible. The gospel is the power of God for salvation (Rm 1:16). Everyone who believes this power-packed message will live forever by faith. What is the content of this message? The NT records various iterations, but the Apostle Paul offered one compact version that I think is very helpful because it is short enough to easily memorize while it carries the essential truths that bring life through belief. It is found in 1 Corinthians 15:3-5:

> 3 For I passed on to you as most important what I also received: that
> Christ died for our sins according to the Scriptures, 4 that he was buried,
> that he was raised on the third day according to the Scriptures, 5 and that
> he appeared to Cephas, then to the Twelve.

Paul offers this brief statement "to make clear...the gospel [he] preached..." It is the message by which Christians "are being saved." This gospel is God's revelation ("according to the Scriptures") about the conflict created by sin, the one appointed to rescue mankind from his certain destruction (Christ), his completed work (death and burial to pay for our sins), and the hope we have that is anchored in the demonstrated power of his own resurrection (affirmed by his appearances).

Are there lots more details? Certainly. And from conversation to conversation different details will need to be shared. But this short version of the gospel helps us keep track of the essential elements that the unbeliever needs to hear. If we leave out the problem of sin, our good news is not really necessary but may only be seen as helpful at best. If we leave out "according to the Scriptures," the gospel may be something we made up just now rather than a revelation of God himself. If we leave out burial, perhaps Jesus only suffered, and the death demanded by sin has not really been met. If we forget about the resurrection on the third day, then where is our hope for our own resurrection? And on it goes.

If you have become a disciple of Jesus, then you must have already heard and believed these essential truths, and these are what you must proclaim to others. And it is self-evident you already have the ability to share what you know to this extent. You will certainly grow to understand these truths more precisely and more deeply, and that will equip you with more precise and deeper ways to share. This itself is a godly desire built into disciples, and you should pursue this growth. Here are some practical ways to become a better herald for your King.

First, read your Bible. Sometimes this is a craving that needs no outside encouragement – *Who wouldn't want to read letters from their true love?* But still, many times Bible reading is a discipline, something we do for our own good regardless of whether we are craving it. Sometimes we are hungry, and other times not so much. But we eat or we die. The same is true for spiritual food. The Bible gives us words of life. It is our spiritual food. The more you read, the more understanding you have to fill in the details in the particular ways they are needed as you talk with people.

There are a multitude of tools to help with Bible reading and study, including many free ones. These help you understand as you read. For example, *systematic theologies* help you understand the major topics or themes of the Bible and give references where to read up on them. These are especially helpful to prepare for or respond to questions seekers ask you. A couple of good ones I recommend are by Wayne Grudem and Millard Erickson, both of which are available in shorter laymen's versions besides the thicker seminary level ones. Grudem's even has related podcasts (web search "grudem systematic theology podcast"). In addition, there are many other resources, such as ligonier.org that deal topically with what the Bible says. Another kind of resource is the *commentary*. Commentaries offer background information and interpretive suggestions by a host of notable biblical scholars. Many are available for purchase in hard copies as well as online. One free commentary I have found extremely useful is offered online with the NET Bible translation provided by bible.org. It is by Thomas Constable, a long-time professor at Dallas Theological Seminary and pastor of Plano Bible Chapel, and it is also available on a separate website (sonicLight.com).

That leads me to a second suggestion. Listen carefully to others. By this I mean those with whom you have opportunity to share the gospel. The better you listen and understand that person's worldview (their system of beliefs to make sense of the world), their struggles and hurts, the better you will be at engaging them with the particulars of the gospel. This listening could mean the difference between confusing them or bringing clarity, between drawing them or offending them, between offering them what they need or frustrating them with what seems like an argument or a sales pitch they don't want.

Many times, especially in what most are now calling a post-Christian culture, a person you engage will not be ready to talk about the gospel until you have helped them realize the inadequacies of a non-Christian worldview. This need is met by a field called Christian Apologetics. Apologetics does not mean apologizing for anything, but rather defending it by means of systematic argumentation and discourse. In other words, it brings a philosophical approach to defending the propositional claims of biblical Christianity. Resources like reasonablefaith.org are helpful here. Many people understand little to nothing of the meaning behind Christian terms, though they may think they do because they have heard them a lot. Asking pointed questions and communicating in basic straightforward language helps you assure the other person understands the truth.

With defending the Christian worldview, I urge caution and offer another practical tip: stay focused. While our culture may demand that the disciple become somewhat of an apologist, we must be careful to not let secondary issues distract us from the real need of those who have not yet trusted Jesus. That need is the gospel. When you begin to share the gospel, someone may begin to ask you questions about politics or hot-button issues of current pop culture. That can easily become a distraction from his or her real need. Paul is helpful again. While he is the one who engaged with the philosophers at the Areopagus with the Greeks who worshiped many gods but not the one true God (Acts 17: 16-31), he still moved from this cultural starting point back toward the essential truths of the gospel (vv. 30-31). He knew *that* is the power of God for salvation for *all*. For us, too, the non-Christian will determine where the conversations *begin*, and we must naturally engage them there, but we know we must bring them from that point *to the gospel*.

Much more could be said, but for now, here is one more practical tip: stay encouraged. It is not unusual for a new convert to be naturally super-charged to want to share the gospel with others. That is not surprising in the least! The Holy Spirit has just brought them to life through this message! However, some personalities do not experience that strong or extroverted of a reaction to conversion at all, and for many others who do, the excitement to proclaim the gospel eventually fades over time. As with Bible reading, how we feel does not change the command of Christ. We are heralds whether we feel like having the conversations or not. Be assured, God will reach out to those he is calling whether we are faithful as heralds or not. But if we keep silent, we miss out on one of the most fundamental things a disciple does, because Jesus' disciples proclaim the gospel.

For this reason, I think it is especially helpful to realize that one guy we might picture as one of the most prolific evangelists ever still seemed to need encouragement. Near the end of Paul's letter to the Ephesian disciples, and even after all the encouragement and exhortation he offered them, he asked them, "Pray also for me, that the message may be given to me when I open my mouth to make known with boldness the mystery of the gospel" (Eph 6:19). He had just encouraged them to pray for their own perseverance, and to pray for each other (v.18). And make no mistake, he is asking for the right *words* to say when his opportunities come – he, Paul, who wrote so much of the NT! But he is also asking for *boldness*. This is the guy who took beatings and nearly died to proclaim Christ asking for boldness! He would need it, for he was going to share the gospel with a king (Acts 26)!

Clearly, Paul wanted us to understand that we do not proclaim the gospel on our own. We need the Spirit to empower and help us. So, however confident or motivated you may or may not feel, pray for boldness and the right words from the Holy Spirit, and then proclaim the gospel.

**Talk it over**

*How would you summarize the gospel in your own words?*

*How does it encourage you to know that as a herald you don't deliver your <u>own</u> message but rather the <u>King's message</u>? How can that reality be a challenge?*

*How will reading the Bible help you be a better herald?*

No matter whether Day 1 or Year 50 of your Christian life, you won't know everything the Bible teaches.

*How can you be confident in sharing the gospel regardless of questions you may not feel qualified to answer well?*

*To whom is it hardest for you to proclaim the gospel? The easiest?*

*What range of responses do you suppose the herald in our illustration might expect as he delivers his message? What range of responses might you expect as you deliver the gospel?*

**Explore**

Take a few minutes together or before your next meeting to check out some of the suggested resources from this section, or any others about which you know. Share which ones you find really helpful, and why.

**Pray**

Take a moment to pray for each other as Paul described. Pray that the Spirit of Christ would embolden each of you and give you the words to say as you proclaim the gospel to others. Pray that you would be discerning to see your opportunities and act on them in faithfulness as disciples.

## Proclamation through Personal Testimony

I said earlier in this chapter that the disciple of Jesus is not less but rather more than a herald. More than just someone delivering the king's message, the disciple knows the king personally and has experienced his kindness. He is a *witness*. The message he delivers is objective truth that will be accepted or rejected. But his own relationship to the king who sends him brings a relational, experiential dimension that gives a subjective power to the herald's message. The gospel may be casually dismissed as a bare statement of fact but is much harder to ignore when delivered by a disciple who is passionately relating how *he* became convinced.

If your favorite newsfeed popped up with a story about someone claiming to have seen Elvis alive and well at your local Burger King, you'd likely roll your eyes and keep scrolling. But if your best friend – who is an Elvis aficionado – came running up to you and swore he himself saw "the King" at that very same burger joint, you might get a little bit curious! Now, this illustration today carries the difficulty of recognizing someone who was last seen at age 42 and would at this writing be nearly 84! But imagine the scenario playing out on August 21, 1977, on the third day since the pop star's burial at Forest Hill Cemetery. And your friend was not an aficionado, but actually a good friend of the singer. Do you think you'd find your friend's declaration intriguing?

Well, for the first generation of Jesus' disciples this was exactly the case, especially for those called *apostles*. These were firsthand witnesses of Jesus' ministry, his message and miracles. They saw the *real* King murdered on a Roman cross, and on the third day after his death and for a few weeks following they saw him alive again (Acts 1:3)! Even those who had Jesus put to death were unwilling witnesses, as they scrambled to concoct a plan to explain away the empty tomb (Mt 28:11-15).

Those early witnesses to Jesus are crucial to the gospel message, especially as you relate it to a skeptic. Jesus himself had said how important those witnesses would be (Acts 1:8). Understand, *your own* role as a witness follows theirs, and it is valuable too. Two important biblical words help us understand that role. The first identifies *you* as a disciple who is proclaiming Jesus and the gospel: you are a *witness*. The second focuses on the personal and experiential nature of what you share as a witness: you offer your *testimony*.

As a witness for Jesus, you can offer your testimony about him from Day 1 since you began following him. I used the term "personal testimony" in the title of this chapter. That is technically a bit redundant, but we often say it this way to emphasize the personal, relational nature of your testimony. That is, you can repeat someone *else's* testimony (e.g., their story they told you, or you read in a book, etc.), but in this resource, I am talking about your relating your own *firsthand* experience with Jesus. To draw from my analogy in ch.3 where you have moved from jury to the witness stand, when you offer testimony it is your own. You are not relating what someone else says about Jesus but telling what *you* have experienced.

Someone may dismiss or write off your testimony, but they cannot falsify or refute it. You know what you know internally, and they cannot change that reality. But they may be drawn by it, even swayed by it. They cannot be won over to Jesus by it alone, but the Holy Spirit certainly uses your testimony as a tool for His work as He awakens the soul and opens the mind. Operating under the Spirit's power and direction, your testimony is powerful.

This is especially clear in the ways the Greek term is used in the book of Revelation. Here, John in ch.12 writes of those who die for their testimony about Jesus. (We get our word "martyr" from the same Greek root for "testimony.") The scene is in heaven, but it tells about victory on earth by God's people over Satan:

> 10 Then I heard a loud voice in heaven say,
> The salvation and the power
> and the kingdom of our God
> and the authority of his Christ
> have now come,
> because the accuser of our brothers and sisters,
> who accuses them
> before our God day and night,
> has been thrown down.
> 11 They conquered him
> by the blood of the Lamb
> and by the word of their testimony;
> for they did not love their lives
> to the point of death.

The very reason that many over the centuries have died and will die for giving their testimony about Jesus is because our enemy knows how powerful it is. By the way, I used the singular form, "testimony," on purpose as that is the form in the verses above. This is because all disciples have – in some sense – the same testimony about Christ. The plural "they" in v.11 above conquered the accuser by the word of their singular testimony. Naturally, all Christian witnesses have different details in their testimony, but the essential story is the same. When we all tell who Jesus is and what he has done for us, the same themes emerge, much like the way I wrote of the plot arc in the last chapter. Together with the objective truth of the written gospel in Scripture this forms a unified testimony about Jesus. It is evident throughout John's book that closes the biblical canon that the testimony is about *Jesus* ("*of* Jesus" – 1:2; 1:9; 10:10; "*about* Jesus" – 12:17; 20:4). In fact, the first words of the book are, "The Revelation of Jesus Christ..." God gave the revelation to Jesus, who made it known to John through an angel, and then John testified in agreement with the word of God and Jesus' own testimony (v.2).

This kind of collaborative testimony happened in the first books of the NT. Four different writers each penned his own gospel account: Matthew, Mark, Luke and John. But since the earliest copies were being distributed these were together referred to as "The Fourfold Gospel." Now, were we to write down *our* own individual testimonies, we could not rightly call them Scripture. Still, they do agree with what these men testify, and indeed with what all of Scripture testifies about Jesus, such that our own personal testimonies are part of the collective testimony about Jesus.

Why do I emphasize this? Because it is important as we proclaim Jesus in this personal and powerful way that we stay focused on the person about whom we testify. If you sat before a jury whose one concern was to determine whether Jesus is worthy of worship and devotion, and all you did was go on and on about yourself, with barely a mention of his name, you'd likely hear, "Thank you, we have no further questions. You may step down. Are there any other witnesses?"

That's not our goal.

As disciples, we want to deliver the good news that transforms, that brings life. When we do, we want to add our own testimony of how we *know* this news is true – because it has transformed *our* lives. Thus, the central person of the *gospel* must be the central person of our *testimony* – Jesus. The old song captures the subjective and personal nature of a disciple's testimony:

> *He lives, he lives! Christ Jesus lives today!*
> *He walks with me and talks with me along life's narrow way.*
> *He lives, he lives, salvation to impart.*
> *You ask me how I know he lives? He lives within my heart!*

So, Jesus' disciples proclaim the gospel as we scatter to our own circles of influence and activity. That means we share the gospel message itself. It also means we share our personal testimony. That is, we offer our firsthand accounts as witnesses to Jesus. We tell his story with our own personal details. We reveal him by telling about his work in our own lives. How can we be not only effective *heralds* but effective *witnesses*? How do we stay focused on the witness stand, especially if we are already nervous in front of the jury? Let me offer a typical and practical outline for your testimony that helps most people.

First, share what you were like before Christ. Be careful here not to accidentally *glorify* your depravity. It doesn't make Christ more glorious the uglier you make your old self. He was perfectly glorious before you existed. What you are trying to get across here is your great need for Jesus, and how nothing or no one else could meet that need. The "jury" – your listeners" – should easily identify with your need and your struggle, even if they don't wear it on their sleeves.

Next, tell them how you came to know and trust Christ, and how that decision to follow him changed everything. You are telling them how a dead person was brought back to life. The propositional truths of the gospel should naturally and easily weave into this story, for this is how Jesus transformed you. What did you come to believe, and how has that changed everything?

Last, explain what life is like now because of Jesus, what he is doing in and through you. This makes sense of why you didn't just zap into Paradise, and why you behave the way you do (more on that in the next chapter), and why you are talking to them about all this stuff anyway. Don't be afraid to be transparent here. The difference now is not that you have everything figured out or all together, but that you now have hope, a Savior and a Helper. You have real power to please God by cooperating with what he is doing in you through Christ.

If you remember that the whole goal is to make a HUGE deal about Jesus, then you'll do fine.

It is often said it is wise to have several versions of your testimony in terms of detail and length – say, a 5-minute version, a 2-minute one and one you could spit out in 30 seconds on an elevator. I think there is some wisdom there, because it helps you stay on track if you've given it some thought.

But more important is to remember your personal testimony is NOT a presentation. Remember, you are more like a witness on the stand than a presenter in a board room. A witness has usually given some thought to how they'll answer likely questions, but if they whip out a white board and start rattling off in monotone something they clearly rehearsed, the jury will probably get very suspicious.

It is quite likely that your testimony will naturally spill out in several places during a conversation, or even over multiple conversations. Don't be freaked out if you don't get to everything in one opportunity – in many cases you should not. Simply realize that when the opportunity comes for you to share how Jesus has saved you and will save you, you have a powerful opportunity to share your particular story as part of the testimony about him. Your unique story is part of a vast, unified and powerful witness to the unique Savior. May God bless you as you tell it!

**Talk it over**

Share your personal testimonies with each other. Talk about and experiment with the shortest version versus more detailed ones.

*What themes do your testimonies share? What details are most different?*

*To what kind of seeker do you think you would relate especially easily? Why?*

*Where would you expect to find common ground between their struggles and your own?*

**Pray and Worship**

Praise God for how he revealed himself to you and how he is transforming you. Thank him for the collective witness of all who have come before so that you could hear their testimony. Ask Jesus to guide you and embolden you to be a faithful and effective witness as you tell others *your* story *about him.*

## Proclamation through Holy Living

I said before that the disciple is more than a *herald*. She is also more than a *witness*. She is a *representative*. And she is a special kind of representative, for she has become a member of the Royal Family. She is doing more than proclaiming the good news of the Kingdom. She is doing more than giving testimony about what the King has done for her personally. She is showing what a *child* of the King looks like in everyday life. What is the culture of this kingdom of Jesus? How do "New Jerusalemites" or "Zionists" live (Rv 3:12; 21:2; cf. Is 52:1-10; ch.60)? In other words, how do Christians live? This is the powerful proclamation of *holy living*.

God set himself apart in the OT as completely unique and utterly good. Then he called to himself a people who would represent his holiness before the world. He told them to be holy as he is holy (Lv 11:44-45; 19:2). The Apostle Peter made it very clear that this old calling was passed on to the NT Church (1 Pt 1:15-16). The disciple of Christ is called to live a holy life, a godly life that shows Jesus off to the outsider who is not yet a citizen of the Kingdom of God. Why is this important?

Credibility.

Suppose you had just spent two hours having a salesman from a new car dealership work himself into a sweat trying to convince you to buy a new Ford. He explains they are the best made, most dependable vehicles, and they have the best warranty and customer service. You are thinking hard about it, nearly convinced, so the salesman has handed you off to talk with someone about financing options. You are barely two minutes into that conversation when you notice the salesman walk out the employee entrance around back and drive off in a new Toyota. Hmm. What do you think of his pitch about the superiority of Fords?

Automobile choices aren't morally right or wrong (of themselves), so let's change the arena. What do you think of a politician who runs on a platform of reform, of cleaning up corruption, who is then exposed to be taking bribes under the table to support her campaign? What is your reaction when it is revealed that a prominent pastor, priest or other religious leader has been secretly living a life of rampant immorality, victimizing others and abusing his position of trust?

*In* – credible. Literally. They make the claims they have propped up to be hard to believe. This is because everyone understands there should be integrity between what someone *says* and what they are *living*. The *lack* of integrity forces one to logically conclude either their message is untrue, or *they* are untrue, at least in those moments of inconsistency.

So it is with disciples of Jesus. We proclaim the gospel, the good message of God that Paul said has the power to save and transform lives (Rm 1:16 with 12:1-2; cf. 2 Cor 3:18). More than that, we offer our personal testimony that this gospel *has* transformed – and *is* transforming – *our own* lives. What is a natural response of those we tell? They watch us to see if this is for real. Integrity, or lack of the same, is what makes the difference between whether our good news is likely to be received as truth or rejected as propaganda.

This is true enough if we were representatives like the salesman or the politician. No one necessarily expects a courier (herald) to live out whatever is on the document she delivers – she's just a messenger. But if she is delivering that message as a *representative* of the company – if the logo is on the uniform or hat – then the expectations rise. She's purporting to be a "satisfied customer" who is recommending the company's services to you. But this is even *more* true if she is the *daughter of the founding president and CEO.*

As disciples of Jesus, we are heralds... and more. We are those who have "tasted that the Lord is good" (1 Pt 2:3). So, we testify. But we are called to even more than this. As children of the king, we are called to live out holy lives as his most important representatives – as his children who bear his image (see chs. 4&5). We carry his name along with his message. He has attached his reputation to ours. So, as we proclaim the gospel message, and as we share our personal testimony, we proclaim our holy God by our own holy living.

Peter, James and John, the three guys Jesus drew into his inner circle among all his disciples, made it very clear how important is our holy living.

James is often recognized as being super practical about this subject in his letter to the scattered Christians of the first century. He challenged them to welcome the kinds of tests that God uses to show their faith to be authentic and to bring it to maturity (Jas 1:2-4). They are to not only *hear* the word of God but to *do it* (vv.22-25). James affirmed the expectation that if someone claims to have faith in God, they should also demonstrate that faith in action (2:14-26). Those with whom you share the gospel have that same expectation.

Probably no one helps us more to understand our calling as *children* of God than John. In ch.3 of his gospel, he records a conversation where Jesus explains to Nicodemus, a ruler and religious leader among the Jews, the spiritual birth from above that brings one into the kingdom of God. Then in ch.8, Jesus talks with a crowd of Jews, almost certainly including religious leaders among them. Here he makes explicit the relationship between the things they do and whose children they are. Those who do the things of God are his children, while those who act like the devil are the devil's children (vv.42-47).

John brings this language into his first letter, where he repeatedly addresses disciples as "children." He uses the language of "walking in the light" to challenge them to make it an ongoing practice to deal with their sin so that they properly show they belong to God. In the end of ch.2 he says,

> **28** So now, little children, remain in him so that when he appears we may have confidence and not be ashamed before him at his coming. **29** If you know that he is righteous, you know this as well: Everyone who does what is right has been born of him.

The children of God must have integrity in their conduct. And John repeatedly points to one particular expression of authentic faith among Christians: that they love one another. I'll say more about that in a moment.

Peter was especially aware of the reality that the disciple is a representative. Remember, he blew it. When the movement to murder Jesus was nearing climax, at the point of Jesus' arrest, Peter was identified as a follower of Jesus among a crowd that was clearly hostile. Peter tried three times to pull back from the association, denying at last that he even knew Jesus (Mt 26:69-75). But talk about transformation! After his resurrection, Jesus restored Peter, and charged him with "feeding [his] sheep" (Jn 21:15-19). And that he did!

In his first letter, Peter could hardly make more explicit why the disciple of Jesus should live a holy life. The Christ-follower has a unique privilege even the angels do not get to enjoy, apart from viewing and celebrating it (1 Pt 1:13). Because we are born into a living hope (vv.3-4), we are called to display God's holiness through our own (vv.13-21). As John said, so Peter affirms that one of the most important ways we show holiness is through loving other Christians (v.22). In ch.2, Peter moves to the function of the disciple's holy living before the non-Christian. He gives a purpose statement that explains the reason we are called out as a holy people is "*so that you may proclaim the praises of the one who called you out of darkness into his marvelous light*" (v.9). We are to "conduct [ourselves] honorably among the Gentiles (non-Christians), *so that...they will observe your good works and will glorify God on the day he visits*" (v.12). Here, Peter acknowledges the likely and often typical response of slander from non-Christians, but he also sees a hopeful possibility: *that "they will...glorify God on the day he visits."* The "day God visits" is used in the Bible negatively to refer to a day of judgment, or positively to refer to a day of mercy. Everyone will bow the knee and glorify God in confessing Jesus as Lord (Rm 14:11; Php 2:10-11), but Peter seems to be aiming at a more robust confession. Certainly, the holy living of God's people vindicates God's glory (see Job 1-2), but that same holy living may bring greater glory to God when it results in the conversion of a lost soul. This hope is what Peter holds out to wives with non-Christian husbands who may be "won over" by the wives' "pure, reverent lives" (3:1-2). It seems likely that hope is imbedded in Peter's purpose statement in 2:12.

When we put all this together, we see that disciples of Jesus have a great opportunity to win others over to him largely through holy living. This works out in two arenas. First, the Christian shows integrity and gives credibility to her message when she lives a godly life *before* the non-Christian. The outsiders watch how she lives and sees if she is truly being transformed. Most importantly they watch to see if she demonstrates love for other Christians.

Second, the Christian lives a godly life *for* the non-Christian. That is, she demonstrates love for them by actions that *involve* them. She reaches out to bring the outsider *into* the experience of Christ's love, so that it is more than something they *observe*, and now something they *experience for themselves*. This is the difference between telling your friend how awesome your new car is versus giving them a ride in it. You can rattle off specs and stats and show them how beautiful it looks, but if you really want them to love this car you will open the door for them to get in and experience it.

We do more than *tell* how great Jesus is. We *show* it. It turns out kindergarten gave the disciple a great tool: *show and tell*. This tool characterizes the integrity the world rightly expects.

One more thing as I close this chapter. Please do not take the challenge of holy living to mean that you must be either A) a perfect Christian or B) a lousy evangelist. Don't worry that the non-Christian will see you screw up – they will. But while screwing up is never a good evangelistic strategy, it is still an opportunity. It is a powerful thing for an outsider to see a Christian *own up* when they *screw up*. How can that be? Because, as I said above, we testify both that Jesus *has transformed* and *is transforming* our lives. Many non-Christians actually misunderstand the gospel – they think our message only includes the first part. So, they wrongly think we now claim to be perfect (1 Jn 1:8-10). That "gospel" would glorify *us*. So, when we give them the *whole* story, that only Christ is perfect, but that even when we screw up God still accepts us in his Son, they see the true gospel. It bothers us when we screw up, not that God will now reject us as no longer his children but because we have offended our holy Father. When the non-Christian sees our brokenness, our humble confession *and* our ongoing confidence in our standing through Christ's goodness (1 Jn 1:9; 2:1-2), then they might consider that *they too* could have that. So, even when we do blow it, we have the opportunity to show the godliness of confession, humility and trust.

**Talk it over**

Think of the stories of God's people throughout the Bible. *How many times are we shown their flaws? Why do you think this is? How does this relate to your opportunity to share and live out the gospel?*

*How does it feel to know God has attached his reputation to yours?*

*In what particular areas do you feel confident you have integrity as a witness? What areas are more challenging for you?*

*How does it help to know that even your failures can be an opportunity for the gospel?*

**Pray and Worship**

Thank God that he is satisfied with you in Christ, even when you are still imperfect.

Pray for each other, asking God to help you share the gospel with the integrity of godly living Pray specifically, drawing from the things you've discussed above.

# Ch.7 Growing and Deepening in the Gospel as They Gather

Disciples are children of God who proclaim to everyone possible the riches of God's kindness expressed to us in Jesus. We show God to the world as we do our best to follow Jesus in living holy lives. These are more than natural things for Christians to do – they are things we are commanded to do. And so, we proclaim and live out the gospel.

We were never meant to do this alone.

After calling them to himself, Jesus lived with his disciples. He certainly had his moments alone and away from them, (e.g., Mt 14:13; 26:36,42,44), but togetherness characterized the disciples throughout their time with Jesus, and that reality continued on after his resurrection and ascension. They were together when they received the Holy Spirit at Pentecost (Acts 2:1-4). They hung together from that point forward, sharing life and gathering together in both large and small groups (vv.44-47). Even in times of persecution throughout Church history, when public assembly has been forbidden, Christians have gathered together as much as they could because they *need* each other. From the start we were designed to be a community.

The NT writers used terms like "building," "household," and "body" to describe the essential nature of our interconnectedness. In fact, the very meaning of the word "church" is "the assembly." Just as with our call to proclaim the gospel, our assembling together is so critical that it is both natural and commanded. The writer of Hebrews told us to "watch out for one another to provoke love and good works," and then to that end he states we should "not [neglect] to gather together," especially "as you see the day (of the Lord) approaching" (10:24-25).

So, while it is imperative for the disciple to go out proclaiming the gospel to make more disciples, it is also crucial that he gathers together with other disciples to "provoke love and good works." When we gather together, many important things happen to help us grow and deepen in our gospel understanding and to practice gospel realities in our relationships with one another. I said in ch.6 that this has a powerful effect on our role as witnesses before the world. It also has a profound effect on each of us internally as we grow to be more like the Christ we proclaim.

So, how do we grow and deepen in the gospel as we gather? First, we rehearse the gospel in various ways. This helps us continue to understand better and better what God has done through Christ. It also helps us avoid falling back into the ditches of *license* – where we wrongly believe we are free to do anything we want – or *legalism* – where we start to live as though we must (or could) please God with our own goodness. When we repeatedly look back at the gospel, we ensure that it is so interwoven into our thinking that we truly live lives of worship as a response (Rm 12:1-2).

## Gospel Rehearsal in Corporate Worship

Think about when a new baby is born to a family. What's the first thing everyone can hardly wait to do? *See* her! Mom, Dad, extended family and friends want to check her out. They hold her, and observe her features – whose eyes, whose nose, whose hair color? They might inspect her from every angle. Not long after, they start to notice and make comments about how even her mannerisms are like one family member's or another's. *What's she doing now?*

Think about a jeweler or a discerning customer inspecting a precious diamond. They look at it *from every angle*, checking out how the light refracts through every facet. They look with their eyes, and then they use *tools* that *magnify* the jewel so they can look even more closely.

Think about a group of adults from grandads and grandmas to little kids gathered around. The older ones reminisce (maybe while playing pitch or hearts or bridge) with story after story about so-and-so, that most memorable family member or friend they all grew up with. The kids soak it in and wish they too could know him! You can see the sparkle in the eyes with every funny or sad anecdote. Everyone longs for the next time they get to see this celebrity!

These illustrations capture some important aspects of what happens when disciples of Jesus gather to worship Jesus together. We keep walking through the gospel, the story of how Jesus is our life. Over and over we look at our Savior's glory to know him better and better. We look at him and his work from every angle, seeing beauty through the light of Scripture. The stories are so amazing, and Jesus is so awesome that we who know him can hardly wait to see him again, and the children are dying to meet him!

What makes the reality even better than the illustrations is that Jesus himself is actually there with us in the gathering through the Holy Spirit, just as we discussed in ch.1.

This is church. Disciples come together so that the Spirit of the living Word (Jesus Christ) will minister to us and through us to one another through the written Word. This is what Paul is talking about in Colossians 3:16 when he writes, "Let the word of Christ dwell richly among you." This "word ministry" results in all the kinds of interpersonal expressions of godliness one would expect among God's people:

> 12 Therefore, as God's chosen ones, holy and dearly loved, put on
> compassion, kindness, humility, gentleness, and patience, 13 bearing
> with one another and forgiving one another if anyone has a grievance
> against another. Just as the Lord has forgiven you, so you are also to
> forgive. 14 Above all, put on love, which is the perfect bond of unity. 15 And
> let the peace of Christ, to which you were also called in one body, rule
> your hearts. And be thankful. 16 Let the word of Christ dwell richly among
> you, in all wisdom teaching and admonishing one another through
> psalms, hymns, and spiritual songs, singing to God with gratitude in your
> hearts. 17 And whatever you do, in word or in deed, do everything in the
> name of the Lord Jesus, giving thanks to God the Father through him.

Disciples focus on God's Word because it is *life* to them (Ps 119:25,107; Jn 6:68). This ministry of the *word* comes through various forms which we will discuss in a moment. But another key understanding of what happens when disciples gather is that it is *spiritual* ministry. Many of the most important things we understand about the church come from Paul, and especially helpful is his letter to the Ephesians. He emphasizes the Spirit-filled nature of our gatherings in ch.5:

> 15 Pay careful attention, then, to how you live—not as unwise people
> but as wise—16 making the most of the time, because the days are evil.
> 17 So don't be foolish, but understand what the Lord's will is. 18 And don't
> get drunk with wine, which leads to reckless living, but be filled by the
> Spirit: 19 speaking to one another in psalms, hymns, and spiritual songs,
> singing and making music with your heart to the Lord, 20 giving thanks

always for everything to God the Father in the name of our Lord Jesus Christ, [21] submitting to one another in the fear of Christ.

Apart from our gathering together under the influence of the Holy Spirit, we will struggle to maintain spiritual, godly lives. We need these regular times together, not only each Sunday (as is typical) with the entire local congregations of Christ-followers but also other times with smaller groups or perhaps one other disciple. However, it is not enough to simply get together. The passages above, and a host of others, make it clear that these gatherings must be centered on God's Word, and filled with and guided by his Spirit.

What should happen in these meetings? Well, not everything happens in every occurrence, but Scripture has prescribed some elements that apparently are to be regularly featured when the *entire local church* gathers. I'll discuss those in the remainder of this first section of ch.7. Then many of those elements find expression in *smaller gatherings* as well, along with other spiritual disciplines. We'll talk about those throughout the rest of this chapter.

"Corporate worship" is a term often used to describe what the church does in the big meetings that usually happen on Sunday morning. Since the Bible is our authority for determining anything we should or shouldn't do, we naturally consult the Scriptures to see what God has prescribed for our corporate worship times. It turns out God was very specific with what he wanted to happen when Israel gathered to worship him in the OT times. He prescribed everything down to the furniture.

But oddly enough, when we look at the NT for what is prescribed for Christ's Church, we are given very few details. We might come to have opinions about things like furniture or musical instrumentation or candles, but God doesn't seem interested in that for us. In fact, many of the churches gathering in the 1st century had none of that. (Many had to meet in the catacombs!) Turns out, the NT emphasis shifts from minutia and details to focus on the spirit and character of the meeting, and only a handful of activities and forms are prescribed. Any elements or forms we might introduce will not be appropriate if they confuse or distract from what God has clearly prescribed by command or principle. A confusing worship service does not reflect well on our God (1 Cor 14:33) and does not benefit the church. But a godly worship service will build up the church (v.26). We might find it useful to do other things that are consistent with the principled demands of the NT, but there are a few things we *must* do with some kind of regularity. *What are those things?*

We might call these *liturgical elements*. These are spiritual disciplines that we are clearly supposed to observe together in our weekly large gatherings. We *read* the word (Col 4:16; 1 Thes 5:27; 1 Tm 4:13). We *sing* the word (Eph 5:19; Col 3:16). We *teach* or *preach* the word (Acts 2:42; 1 Cor 14:19; Eph 4:11-13; Col 3:16; 2 Tm 4:2). We *pray* the word (Mt 6:9-13; 21:13; Acts 2:42; Eph 6:18; 1 Thes 5:17; 1 Tm 2:1; Jas 5:16). Praying is speaking to God from a position of humility, thankfulness and dependence, where we praise him and ask for his help and his direction. In addition to these activities, we *give offerings* to support the ongoing ministries of the church that are centered on the word (Acts 4:32-35; 1 Cor 9:14; 16:1-2; 2 Cor 9).

When you come to worship with a local church on a typical Sunday, these things should be happening. If they are not, find another church. Remember, the *Word of God* is *life* (Ps 119:25,107; Jn 6:68), and his *Spirit* is life (v.63). This is why Jesus taught that the Father looks for those who worship him in Spirit and in truth (Jn 4:23-24). Like the Samaritan woman of John 4, we may easily get caught up in arguments over locations (and trappings and décor), but a true worship gathering will focus on Spirit and truth and will find expression in the forms of ministry mentioned above.

Our liturgy is to be designed around the word of God, and specifically, it is focused on rehearsal of all the rich facets of the gospel as it works in us. Our teaching must not degenerate into religious moralism. Our songs must exalt the Father, Son and Spirit and focus on gospel themes. Our prayers must be gospel prayers. This will keep our lives gospel-centered in our gatherings and as we leave them to go proclaim the gospel to the world.

There are two other liturgical elements that are clearly commanded for the church to observe when gathered. I include them separately here only because they may not occur in every weekly church gathering. We call these biblical *ordinances*. This word simply means they are ordained or appointed directly by Jesus for the church to practice.

One of them is believer's *baptism*. I have said the first urgent calling for a disciple from Day 1 is to proclaim the gospel. I have also said even the brand-new convert can share her testimony. A simple and very powerful way to do both is through baptism. This is a symbolic ritual commanded by Jesus

(Mt 28:19), where we identify with him by immersion in water. The symbolism directs the practice. Jesus died once for all sins (Rm 6:10; 1 Pt 3:18), so we are baptized once. After his death Jesus was entombed, so we are immersed completely in water. In the power of the Holy Spirit Jesus raised to life on the third day, so we are raised out of the water to new life in Christ (though we don't have to wait three days!).

As I said in ch.6, all disciples have the same testimony in some sense. That common testimony is what we express through baptism. We all show that our old lives are dead and buried with Christ, and that we are raised to a new life in his own resurrection (Rm 6:4-11). Now, many churches encourage people to share the personal aspects of their testimony just before they are baptized (perhaps via a prepared video), but the symbolic ritual carries the powerful images of the testimony we all share.

Given all I have just said about what biblical baptism is, it should be clear why I used the qualifier in saying this ordinance is *believer's* baptism. The NT pattern is consistent that the command for baptism is for those who have put their trust in Jesus for salvation from sins.

The other biblical ordinance for the church was also commanded by Jesus himself. It is usually called *communion* or *the Lord's table*. Just before his arrest and crucifixion, Jesus excitedly took a most prominent Jewish feast as an opportunity to institute this new ritual. He told his disciples he "fervently desired to eat this Passover" with them before he would suffer on the cross (Lk 22:15). The Passover was a centuries-old celebration of how God delivered his people out of their bondage to the Egyptians through the last plague recorded in Exodus 12. What saved God's people was the sacrifice of the Passover Lamb. This symbol was so important God commanded the Israelites to commemorate the occasion year after year (vv.24-27). Jesus, a Jew himself, would naturally want to gather with his closest friends for this momentous feast. But he did something new.

Jesus took the symbol of the Passover Lamb and applied it to himself. As he shared the meal with his disciples, he connected the dots for them:

Luke 22:19–20

[19] And he took bread, gave thanks, broke it, gave it to them, and said,
"This is my body, which is given for you. Do this in remembrance of me."
[20] In the same way he also took the cup after supper and said, "This
cup is the new covenant in my blood, which is poured out for you.

So, Jesus radicalized the Passover celebration and commanded his disciples to perpetuate this new ritual that was really a fulfillment of the old – Jesus would become the ultimate Passover Lamb that would save lives eternally. The purpose for the ordinance is clear: it is a commemoration. Disciples come together to remember what Jesus accomplished in offering his body and blood for our sins.

Further, it is clear that this commemoration was meant to be observed by the church until Jesus returns. Paul echoes Jesus and confirms the tradition was passed on to him and through him to the church:

1 Corinthians 11:23–26

[23] For I received from the Lord what I also passed on to you: On the
night when he was betrayed, the Lord Jesus took bread, [24] and when he
had given thanks, broke it, and said, "This is my body, which is for you.
Do this in remembrance of me."
[25] In the same way also he took the cup, after supper, and said, "This
cup is the new covenant in my blood. Do this, as often as you drink it, in
remembrance of me." [26] For as often as you eat this bread and drink the
cup, you proclaim the Lord's death until he comes.

As with baptism, the power of the Lord's Table is in the symbols. Every time the church observes this ordinance, we reenact the sacrificial event that triggers all gospel realities. It is the death of Christ for sins that triggers the inheritance of life and blessing for all believers (Heb 9:15-16).

So, if the symbols of baptism and communion are so powerful, why don't we observe them every week? Well, in the case of baptism, the reality is that if there are no new believers there are no baptisms. So, while it is a great sign of God's working through effective evangelism, most local congregations do not see new converts every week. But whenever we do have new professions of faith, we ought to have baptisms.

In the case of communion, local congregations have to struggle with how often seems appropriate for them. Some do practice this ordinance every week. Others find monthly or bi-monthly heightens the importance of the event. Still others may practice it quarterly, often with a whole service devoted to the ritual. Jesus didn't say how often to share this commemoration, and Paul gives no indication of frequency either. The point is that the Lord's Table is a vital part of our corporate worship that should be regularly practiced.

In concluding this section let me point out that the two ordinances are uniquely corporate. That is, both necessarily involve multiple people. They are powerful proclamations that we share with one another, and they are most appropriate in the context of the full assembly.

In the next sections, we will look at gospel ministry that finds expression in both the large and smaller group settings.

**Talk it over**

Some have said things like, "I prefer to worship God on my own out in nature (like on a hike or while golfing)."

*What positive value might be expressed in this kind of statement?*

*How would this limited of a view of worship be inadequate according to the NT?*

*How have you experienced (or would you expect to experience) greater struggles when trying to be godly without the help of others?*

*Have you been in or watched a church worship time that you think fell short of the NT standards? If so, what was it like?*

Read 1 Cor 11:17-22 and 27-32.

*How should we prepare to approach our times of communion? What should this tell us about how to approach every church gathering?*

**Apply It**

*Are you a disciple of Jesus but have never experienced believer's baptism?* If you have never been baptized, if you have experienced a different form of baptism or a baptism prior to understanding and believing the gospel, I encourage you to talk with a pastor about making this important symbolic declaration of your faith in Jesus.

**Pray and Worship**

Thanksgiving is woven throughout everything the NT says about worship. Thank God that he has given you the community of the church to help you grow and deepen in the gospel as you worship together.

## Gospel Learning through Teaching and Equipping

Besides rehearsing the gospel when we gather, we also learn more about it. We learn to understand it better, and we learn the deeper doctrines that flow from it. As we do, we become better equipped to express the gospel in our actions toward one another and in our proclamation to those outside the church.

To draw from my initial workplace illustration, if we want to become the best possible employees, we need training. We need someone to take us through the employee handbook and help us understand policies and best practices. We need to ask questions of veteran employees, and many times a most helpful way to learn is to come under a mentor's tutelage to watch and emulate them. When we get this instruction and training, we function well in the company, and we represent our employer well in the community.

For the disciple of Jesus, teaching and equipping are centered around the truths of Scripture (2 Tim 3:16). Just like in the workplace, these come in various settings. Because they are so important, they are regular features of the Sunday gatherings of most congregations. However, they occur in many other settings too. *Teaching* and *equipping* are biblical terms that express roles performed by those who have some maturity, understanding and skill. In more formal settings, like a church service or a Sunday School class, those who teach and equip other Christians are usually exercising a *spiritual gift*, a special capacity to carry out this work that has been given to them by the

Holy Spirit. I'll discuss more at length about spiritual gifts a little later, but for now, let's focus on the critical work that is accomplished in these two related areas.

A primary passage for helping us understand how the disciple grows in these ways is found in Ephesians 4:

> 11 And he himself gave some to be apostles, some prophets, some
> evangelists, some pastors and teachers, 12 equipping the saints for the
> work of ministry, to build up the body of Christ, 13 until we all reach unity
> in the faith and in the knowledge of God's Son, growing into maturity
> with a stature measured by Christ's fullness. 14 Then we will no longer be
> little children, tossed by the waves and blown around by every wind of
> teaching, by human cunning with cleverness in the techniques of deceit.
> 15 But speaking the truth in love, let us grow in every way into him who
> is the head—Christ. 16 From him the whole body, fitted and knit together
> by every supporting ligament, promotes the growth of the body for
> building up itself in love by the proper working of each individual part.

Now, this passage was written during a time when there were apostles (leaders commissioned directly by Jesus himself) and prophets (those who were given a message directly from God to communicate to his people). The apostles reiterated the things Jesus taught them as they followed him during his earthly ministry (Mt 28:19-20; Acts 2:42). That was a foundational period for the church (Eph 2:20). As those teachings were codified in their writings, these special offices and roles gave way to the primacy of the Bible as the sufficient communication of God for us. Now that we have the complete canon of Scripture, the emphasis is on proclaiming (evangelists), shepherding (pastors) and teaching to equip and build up the church. Teaching and equipping help Christians become unified, to know Christ better and to grow into maturity (v.13 above). Apart from them, individual disciples are in danger of being easily led astray into wrong teachings, or *doctrines* (v.14).

Just as the role of the apostles was foundational in the early development of the church, the teaching and equipping roles today provide the foundation for the other expressions of growing and deepening in the gospel, expressed here as "the work of ministry" that "build[s] up the body of Christ." We need our church gatherings – whether on Sunday mornings, or in a weekday Bible study class, a home-based small group or one-on-ones in a coffee shop – we need these times together when someone who has applied themselves to learning the Scriptures can help us do the same. We are all to be learners.

Now, when we think of teaching and equipping, the picture that often comes into our minds is one expert in front of a crowd delivering wisdom and insight to all. Perhaps it looks like a session with a motivational speaker, or a college lecture. Or maybe you picture some pastor you know, probably who has a title like Teaching Pastor, or Lead Pastor or Senior Pastor. Certainly, for hundreds of years a primary method of teaching in the church has been the "pulpit," where one studious, articulate and (hopefully) engaging speaker teaches the congregation on Sunday. But as I stated in the paragraph above, there are many other forms in which teaching and equipping occur among gathered disciples. We do well to not only commit to weekly sitting under the teaching of the Bible on Sunday but to also pursue these other learning opportunities – we need them.

Yes, we are all to be learners. But we are also all to become teachers, at least in some sense. For most, that won't mean teaching the whole congregation or even a class, but we are *all* called to pass on to others what we have learned. That is inherent in the command from which this resource is titled, the command to *make disciples.* Most of us will do that teaching in the context of only one or a few other Christians. Most of the time it happens very naturally, in dialogue and discussion rather than in a strict teacher/learner situation where most of the communication is in one direction.

The point is that however it is done, the doctrines of the Bible must be intentionally, carefully and accurately passed from one generation of the church to another. That process involves *you.* This is no different from grandad offering pointers while dad is teaching his son about the best ways to perform some handy life skill. Or it is like grandma prompting mom to add a smidge more of some ingredient as she shows her daughter how to make the best pie according to the family recipe. Those who have learned through teaching and experience pass on what they know to those coming behind to help them avoid getting it wrong.

This happens when disciples gather together. It happened with Paul and Timothy. Timothy had training in the Christian faith from an early age by his grandmother and mother (2 Tm 1:5). Paul saw his potential and took him under his wing and trained him skillfully (vv.6,13). Then he charged Timothy with doing the same for others (2:1-2; 4:1-5). The principle is often taught, and rightfully so: everyone has a "Paul," and everyone has a "Timothy." We are all learners, and we all become teachers in some capacity. Your "Timothy" may be your friend, or your child or it could even be someone much older than you. Whomever it may be, look for them, and start sharing what you've learned. For I have found that you never learn something so well as you do when you pass that learning on by teaching it to another.

Notice that what is to be transferred through the generations is biblical truth and training for godliness. Each generation and culture have their own forms and expressions and traditions. These trappings must be held loosely, and many will give way to new expressions in coming generations. But the core, the essentials, must be held sacred and must be transferred, even as they are practiced in new contexts. There is rarely a greater source of conflict in a local congregation than the confusing of these categories. Churches will fight and split over "chocolate and vanilla" issues like furniture, carpet, music styles and programs, while neglecting things like love, unity, service and biblical fidelity. The truth is that congregations can – and probably should – look very different in non-essential ways while being very much the same in core values. Teaching and equipping helps ensure this.

So, disciples gather together to grow and deepen in the gospel. We place ourselves in a position to learn, whether from a pastor delivering the word in front of the whole congregation, from a conversation in a small group where we sharpen one another through dialogue or from a close friend giving a loving, careful and biblical answer over a latte as we pour out our souls over a current struggle. Further, we do more than learn truth as we gather. We are equipped to minister to one another, to build one another up in our faith. This equipping is God's doing, but it is worked out in and through us as we gather (Heb 13:20-21). Particular teaching and equipping gifts are commonly featured in the largest of our gatherings, but any time disciples come together is an opportunity for learning and equipping. It is a natural way we grow and deepen in the gospel.

**Talk it over**

Share something that has been passed down to you by a family member or mentor (like the recipes or skills in the illustration).

*What are the benefits of learning in community versus learning alone (like through reading a book by yourself)?*

Describe a setting where you came to better understand a biblical truth (e.g., a Sunday message, a small group discussion, a service opportunity like a mission trip, etc.). *What was that truth you came to better understand?*

In simply answering that last question, you were active in a form of teaching. Discuss the variety of ways you can learn from or teach another person about the Christian faith.

*Do you think God might have gifted you to teach and equip others in an official capacity (e.g., class teacher, discussion group leader, etc.)? If so, are you currently doing so?*

## Gospel Dependence through Prayer and Accountability

Community is very important for the disciple for many reasons. Beyond rehearsing the gospel and deepening in it through teaching and equipping, we share each other's needs and joys. We rely on one another to help ensure we stay on what Jesus called the "difficult way" of his disciples (Mt 7:13-14). In fact, "the Way" apparently became a kind of shorthand for antagonists referring to a Christian in the first century (Acts 9:2; 24:14,22). Jesus himself is the narrow gate that leads to life, and because he knew the way from there was difficult, he gave us each other for support. As we learned earlier, this support must be empowered by God's Spirit and centered on God's Word. So, we encourage one another to depend upon God as we depend upon one another. Two important ways we do this are through praying together and holding each other accountable.

Now, I have already mentioned that prayer is an important part of the large gathering of the whole local congregation. Remember I defined prayer as speaking to God from a position of humility, thankfulness and dependence, where we praise him and ask for his help and his direction. These prayers, like all prayer, are directed by God's Spirit and his Word toward accomplishing his purposes in his Church. This is why we follow Jesus' model prayer in asking that the Father's will would be done here in us as it is in heaven (Mt 6:9-13). But when we pray publicly in a crowd of dozens, hundreds, or even thousands, it is difficult to both be specific and to represent everyone in the congregation. On the other hand, when we pray alone, though this is a most intimate time with our loving Father, we do not have the benefit of sharing this experience in bonding with other Christians. We might easily become self-centered.

This is why we desperately need to pray together in smaller groups. When we hear another's needs or joys, we are drawn together with them in seeking God's help or in celebrating his goodness. This honors God doubly as we follow both his command to pray and his command to love one another. There is a richness that is gained by hearing someone else pour out her heart to God. You are drawn into her perspective. You learn her struggles, her fears and her joys. Much of this begins to happen even with the preamble to praying, the moments when we ask one another how we can pray for them. Many times, when I have reached out in this way, I have learned something I had no idea was going on in a brother's or sister's life. So, then I not only can pray more specifically, but I can express a genuine concern for them. Often, we may offer encouragement from a similar circumstance through which God has already brought us. Prayer is an opportunity to say, "God is with you through this, and so am I." Likewise, when another disciple is celebrating good news, we rejoice with them (Rm 12:10-15; 1 Cor 12:26).

So, how do we pray? The model prayer from Jesus mentioned above helps us understand the driving values. Prayer is not our mechanism for getting God to do what we want. Rather, it is our humble approach to him to learn and cooperate with what *he* wants. We approach him as a loving Father (Mt 6:9). We want *him* to be honored. We want *his* will to be done (v.10). This means everywhere and by everyone and everything – most pointedly, us! We depend on him for everything (v.11). Most importantly, we depend upon his forgiveness (v.12) and deliverance (v.13). All of these things are provided through Jesus (Eph 1:3).

Someone has offered a short acronym to help us remember important things to include in our times of prayer. There are a variety of similar tools to help us practice biblical prayer, but I'll offer this one here. Think of the acronym ACTS. The "A" is for adoration. This is simply worshiping God for who he is, a common practice in the OT prayer book we know as the Psalms. "C" is for confession. This is coming to agreement with what God says about himself and about us and especially about our sin. "T" is for thanksgiving. This is a fundamental attitude of prayer and worship that works out in our listing specific things for which we are thankful to him. And "S" is for supplication. This is a term that refers to making requests. Of course, we ask God for things on our own behalf, but we are called to make supplication for others as well, and this is especially important in these small gatherings of two or a few that are the primary concern of this section.

You might be wondering if confession really belongs in this small group context. We know "confession is good for the soul" even from conventional wisdom. And the OT wisdom literature certainly promoted it, saying, "The one who conceals his sins will not prosper, but whoever confesses them will find mercy" (Prv 28:13). *But, isn't confessing sin a personal thing between you and God?* This is true. It is also true that Christ is our mediator when we approach God, so that we don't need any other human to intercede for us to be forgiven by God (1 Tm 2:5; Heb 7:26-27; 10:19-22). But there is an aspect of confession that is very appropriate for disciples. OT wisdom promoted this aspect as well. The Teacher in the book of Ecclesiastes said this:

> [9] Two are better than one because they have a good reward for their efforts. [10] For if either falls, his companion can lift him up; but pity the one who falls without another to lift him up.

That brings me to the other subject in this section, accountability.

In the context of Christ's once-for-all high priestly work that is mentioned in Heb 10 above, the writer goes on to encourage followers of Jesus to "watch out for one another to provoke love and good works" (v.24). We must be around one another in intimate enough settings to know how each other is doing. We want other disciples to succeed. We must know them well enough to help. This kind of collaboration requires communication and transparency. I think this is what John is talking about when he calls the believer to "walk in the light" in 1 John. As I mentioned in ch.6, this whole letter is laced with themes of fellowship and brotherly love as the Christian lives in the light of Christ. It is in that context that John writes his famous verse on confession:

> 5 This is the message we have heard from him and declare to you: God
> is light, and there is absolutely no darkness in him. 6 If we say, "We have
> fellowship with him," and yet we walk in darkness, we are lying and are
> not practicing the truth. 7 If we walk in the light as he himself is in the
> light, we have fellowship with one another, and the blood of Jesus his
> Son cleanses us from all sin. 8 If we say, "We have no sin," we are
> deceiving ourselves, and the truth is not in us. **9 If we confess our sins,
> he is faithful and righteous to forgive us our sins and to cleanse
> us from all unrighteousness.** 10 If we say, "We have not sinned," we
> make him a liar, and his word is not in us.

Understand, there was only one once-for-all atoning sacrifice to pay for our sins (2:2). And Jesus is our one advocate with the Father (v.1). But I believe John pulls in the community of the church to the context of confession for the sake of walking in the light. His discussion about dealing with sin and walking in the light is an evidence of fellowship with God (v.6 above), but it is also associated with fellowship with one another (v.7). I do not claim it is John's main point about confession, but I would argue it is consistent with the theology of this letter that we involve others to some level in our own struggles with sin. This is a key way we love one another.

A brother or sister in Christ doesn't need to know the most intimate details such as we will confess directly to God. Still, we need another person – or better, several others – who can look us in the eye and ask hard questions. We need to trust another human with enough information that they can pray for what challenges us most. We need to give them permission to circle back and see how we're doing. This is one of our most valuable tools for living a holy life that glorifies God – a community to which we are accountable. We should welcome it and depend upon it, remembering that the way another Christian helps us is to point to Christ in these struggles. Seek out fellow disciples who will genuinely care for you in this way. Look for someone you are convinced wants to live holy themselves, and who wants that for you. It is important to pick someone you respect, so that the accountability serves as a real deterrent when you are tempted to sin. If you begin to share real struggles with another disciple, you might be surprised to find out he is craving the help of accountability partners too. It is a powerful thing to realize you are not the only one dealing with an issue.

We tend to see accountability in a negative light. Many people are familiar with the term "church discipline" but only associate it with the most severe step prescribed by Jesus in Mt 18:17. The reality is that the goal of restoring a fellow Christian to a right relationship is accomplished many times over in the positive response to one of the first steps of this process (vv.15-16). But far better is to invite others in and avoid sin altogether. That, in fact, was the result of an accountability group among church staff men with which I was involved. We met weekly for the sake of confession, accountability and mutual prayer support. The result was that our sessions had much more to do with *prevention* than with *damage control* or *cleanup*. Simply welcoming accountability and prayer through transparency accomplishes a huge amount of the work, especially when it becomes a habit. We end up walking in the light like John says.

We need prayer and accountability in the same way we need to regularly maintain our cars. If we routinely check fluid levels, change our oil and filter, maintain recommended tire pressure and so on, we will save ourselves a lot of unnecessary break-downs at the side of the road. But if we never pop the hood, never replace worn or defective parts and ignore warning lights, we are heading for disaster.

Far too many people are content to show up occasionally on a Sunday, act as though everything is fine and try to keep muddling through on their own. That is not God's design for his church. Disciples need each other because we all have struggles and joys. We are easily overcome if we struggle alone, and joys are quickly diminished if we do not share them. We must help one another depend upon God through prayer and accountability.

**Talk it over**

*Have you – or has someone close to you – ever neglected preventative maintenance on a vehicle or appliance or some other equipment? What was the result?*

*In 1 Jn 1:9, what two things does John say result from confession?*

*Could eternal life be gained, lost and then regained? If so, then how would it be eternal? If not, then what is the function of confession of sin AFTER one has eternal life? How is coming in repentance to Christ for the once-for-all forgiveness of sins different from the ongoing spiritual discipline of confession?*

**Pray and apply it**

If you already have accountability partners, thank God for how he is already working through them to help you be faithful and to avoid stumbling. And for those for whom you are an accountability partner (which may or may not be the same people), pray for them now in the specific needs and or joys they have shared with you.

If you do not yet have any accountability partners, think and pray about who God in his wisdom knows would best encourage and spur you to holiness. Then, as he makes it clear, approach them and ask them if they are willing to commit to that relationship. If they are not available for this, do not be discouraged but keep asking God until you find this much needed help.

## Gospel Service through Stewardship and Spiritual Gifts

As we move further into these disciplines you might notice a lot of overlap. That is because the church is an organism. Just like we as people have distinguishable parts but are each a unified whole person, so these disciplines are distinguishable but function as the whole of the disciple's communal and individual life. This means that as we discuss particular disciplines you will quickly notice that they are at work in other disciplines as well. In the last section we talked about depending upon one another in prayerful and accountable relationships. Before that, we covered the teaching and equipping ministries in the church. More than simply interactions, these are ways we *serve* one another. Service is the meaning underneath the word "ministry."

Many people have the idea that ministers are the small percentage among church members who are financially supported staff, but the reality is that every Christian is a minister. That is, every disciple is commanded to "serve one another through love" (Gal 5:13). Since we all have this command, it is a good thing to know that God has given every one of us some kind of unique set of capacities with which to obey. The Apostle Peter calls this a gift that comes from the beautifully diverse grace of God. In 1 Pt 4:7-11 he says this:

> [7] The end of all things is near; therefore, be alert and sober-minded for prayer. [8] Above all, maintain constant love for one another, since **love covers a multitude of sins.** [9] Be hospitable to one another without complaining. [10] Just as each one has received a gift, use it to serve others, as good stewards of the varied grace of God. [11] If anyone speaks, let it be as one who speaks God's words; if anyone serves, let it be from the strength God provides, so that God may be glorified through Jesus Christ in everything. To him be the glory and the power forever and ever. Amen.

Notice the *purpose* of the gift is to *serve others*. Peter calls us stewards of our gifts. Stewardship is a helpful term for the disciple of Jesus to keep perspective. We are only stewards – not owners – of every possible opportunity to serve others. Some summarize this stewardship in terms of our time, our treasure and our talents. Whatever categories we use, we must realize that the only thing we *own* is our stewardship. We do not ultimately determine our resources or capacities. God does that (though we can certainly maximize them through our own diligence). He is the source for all things, and he is the fountain of all capacity. He decides how to distribute these to people. Then from that point, it is our choice to use these as he intended, to show his grace to others by serving them in love.

And notice that *each one* has received a gift. No one is left out. You may not feel like you have anything remarkable or significant to offer in service to anyone, but you do in fact have some gift to offer. Jesus frequently pointed out small offerings that had huge significance. In Mk 9:41, he tells his disciples, "*whoever gives you a cup of water to drink in my name, because you belong to Christ – truly, I tell you, he will never lose his reward.*" The size of the offering is not important to Jesus, but rather the proportion and spirit of the stewardship. This is why he noticed the poor widow's offering above those of the rich in Mk 12:41-44. He said, "*this poor widow has put more into the treasury than all the others. For they all gave out of their surplus, but she out of her poverty has put in everything she had – all she had to live on.*" In truth, everyone's resources are limited. And everyone has the same opportunity to give everything in service. How someone treats her money when the offering plate comes by in a church service is important. But more important is how she treats all the rest of her resources in every opportunity. Does she focus on herself as though she is the owner? Or does she see another Owner, and consider what He wants her to do for others with what He has given her? This is stewardship, and if affects everything God has given us. We are stewards of an hour just as much as we may steward a million dollars. We can serve with a kind word and gentle spirit as powerfully as we might with a powerful sermon or beautiful song.

And notice, too, that even our strength to serve well as a steward comes from God. Peter indicates in the above passage that even our attitude about our stewardship is a stewardship! By saying, "*let it be from the strength God provides,*" he implies that we could serve proudly, thinking much of ourselves for doing it. Peter steers us away from this, calling us to recognize God in every aspect of our service, "*so that God may be glorified through Jesus Christ in everything.*" Remember what we said from the beginning, that God is the only Boss deserving of praise from everyone for everything. All the credit goes to him for what he has done through his Son, Jesus Christ.

The Apostle Paul, like Peter, affirms that every disciple of Jesus has gifts to use in loving service to others. In Romans 12, he summarizes the whole life of a believer as a presentation of ourselves to God to do whatever pleases him. He calls our stewardship a "living sacrifice" (v.1). In this, we follow Christ's pattern as he came to earth to serve the Father by serving humanity with his whole life – even to the point of death. We follow after Jesus by serving one another with diverse and unique expressions of his grace. Paul writes:

> 3 For by the grace given to me, I tell everyone among you not to think
> of himself more highly than he should think. Instead, think sensibly, as
> God has distributed a measure of faith to each one. 4 Now as we have
> many parts in one body, and all the parts do not have the same function,
> 5 in the same way we who are many are one body in Christ and
> individually members of one another. 6 According to the grace given to

> us, we have different gifts: If prophecy, use it according to the proportion of one's faith; 7 if service, use it in service; if teaching, in teaching; 8 if exhorting, in exhortation; giving, with generosity; leading, with diligence; showing mercy, with cheerfulness.

Paul emphasizes the diversity of the gifts with which we serve one another but also the unity of the body of Christ (the church) that is realized through our diversity. Just as our physical bodies are healthy and function well as each different body part performs its unique function, so it is with the body of Christ.

In 1 Corinthians 12, Paul emphasizes this unity in diversity through *spiritual* gifts:

> **12** Now concerning spiritual gifts: brothers and sisters, I do not want you to be unaware. 2 You know that when you were pagans, you used to be enticed and led astray by mute idols. 3 Therefore I want you to know that no one speaking by the Spirit of God says, "Jesus is cursed," and no one can say, "Jesus is Lord," except by the Holy Spirit.
>
> 4 Now there are different gifts, but the same Spirit. 5 There are different ministries, but the same Lord. 6 And there are different activities, but the same God produces each gift in each person. 7 A manifestation of the Spirit is given to each person for the common good: 8 to one is given a message of wisdom through the Spirit, to another, a message of knowledge by the same Spirit, 9 to another, faith by the same Spirit, to another, gifts of healing by the one Spirit, 10 to another, the performing of miracles, to another, prophecy, to another, distinguishing between spirits, to another, different kinds of tongues, to another, interpretation of tongues. 11 One and the same Spirit is active in all these, distributing to each person as he wills.

Paul gets more specific here, in saying that God distributes spiritual gifts through his own Spirit. These gifts are expressed through "*different activities*" for the "*common good,*" and Paul's emphasis here is on spiritual good through spiritual activities. In addition to 1 Pt 4:11 and Rm 12 above, this is another of several places where such gifts are listed (see also vv.28-

30 and Eph 4:11). Clearly, these lists are not comprehensive but a sampling. Further, they include some expressions (like tongues or performing of miracles) that many believe were limited to the times of the early apostles. But the point is that every disciple of Jesus has been given stewardship of some spiritual gifts. We do well to give some thought to our own unique way to build up the church. We are unique not only in our combination of gifts, but in what we have learned and what we have experienced. We are stewards of all these things. *What is your unique combination of spiritual gifts?* There are tools that can help you discover that, and these can be of some use (some links are offered at the end of this section). Keep in mind that as man-made tools these are limited and cannot provide the whole perspective on the ways God will call you to serve. Most important is to see and grow into the opportunities that God puts before us. We must serve one another with these gifts, to build each other up in our faith in Christ. This is an ongoing expression of the gospel in the church. We continue to deepen and grow in what Christ has done for us and is doing in us as we serve one another through spiritual gifts.

More often than not, God seems to present us with opportunities to steward our gifts in situations that play to our strengths. However, sometimes the complete opposite is true. When God called Moses to speak on his behalf before Pharaoh, Moses shied away from the calling because he said he wasn't good at speaking (Ex 4:10). Sometimes, as in this case, God may call us to serve from our weakness, so his own work is even more powerfully on display. Regardless of whether God calls us to serve from our strongest gifting or in situations where we feel sorely inadequate, his call is to *opportunities* more than to displays of gifts for their own sake. Further, it is not unusual for us to find that our unique gifting has shifted somewhat over time as God has refined us and helped us adapt in various situations. Your strongest gifts will likely remain much the same, but you may well find that you grow in some other gifts too.

What does stewardship look like? As we have seen, there is a great amount of diversity in this. Of course, a most direct and practical kind of stewardship is giving material offerings. The primary NT pattern for this is giving to, for and through the local church (Acts 4:34ff; Rm 15:25-29; 1 Cor 16:1-2). In most cases, this means putting money in an offering plate on a Sunday or giving electronically online. But it might also mean donating assets (like automobiles or houses) to the local church or to a foundation that supports a church. Of course, many individuals, ministries or projects that function in cooperation with or distinct from a local church (e.g., foreign missionaries, parachurch organizations or humanitarian ministries) are worthy of support as well. However, the NT seems to indicate our *primary* responsibility is to support our local church. In this, Paul encourages us to give regularly, to give in proportion to how God is prospering us (1 Cor 16:2 above) and to joyfully reflect God's generosity in our own generosity (2 Cor 9:6ff). Giving is a discipline for every Christ-follower. What's more, you should expect that just as the widow lady Jesus observed, you will likely be moved to stretch your gifts beyond what is surplus or comfortable.

But stewardship takes many other forms too. It happens when a gifted pastor explains God's Word to the whole congregation on a Sunday morning, or when a skilled musician leads people to sing songs of praise to God. It may mean taking a meal to someone in your small group who is recovering from surgery. Or it may mean inviting someone over for dinner or taking them out for coffee to get to know them and see how you can help them grow in faith. It might happen anywhere, anytime. Our gifts are for the church, and will surely be expressed when the church gathers, but we also steward opportunities in all kinds of places and situations. We might honor God with our gifts at a ballgame or in a line at the DMV (a couple of really challenging places for some of us to be spiritual!). It may mean giving a car ride to someone who has had too much to drink. The list goes on and on.

Whatever the expression, this is what disciples do. We honor God by being good stewards of every kind of gift he gives us, especially spiritual gifts. We find our unique way to serve others in love in the unified church body. For if we each do not steward well on our part, something will be missing or deficient. But if we serve well, we have joy in participating in a healthy body.

**Resources**

For helpful tools, consider ChurchGrowth.org or Spiritualgiftstest.com or simply google "spiritual gifts test" for many more options. Many such websites will ask for an email address to respond with results. If you prefer not to do that, downloadable PDF's are available at sites like Lifeway.com.

**Talk it over**

*Have you thought before about spiritual gifts, maybe even taken an assessment? What do you think are your strongest gifts? How are you "wired" by God for ministry?*

Sometimes it helps define something by what it is <u>not</u>. *What do think are likely NOT your strongest gifts?*

*Beyond spiritual gifts, what opportunities do your education, experiences, skills and passions offer for you to serve others?*

**Pray**

As we learned, God has given you gifts for his glory and for others' benefit. Thank him for his generosity and grace in this. Be as specific as possible. If this is the first you've really given thought to your gifts, ask God to help you discover how he has wired you for ministry. Beyond that, ask him to help you see every opportunity he gives you, and to give you the desire to follow through for his glory.

## Gospel Fellowship: Christians Living Together in Love and Unity

As I mentioned in the last section, these categories of gospel reality overlap a great deal. This is especially true in this last section of ch.7, where I will discuss fellowship. The concept of fellowship is distinct from worship, teaching and equipping, prayer and accountability and from stewardship and spiritual gifts. Yet, to work toward defining the term, everything I have said in this chapter about these other subjects would give a cumulative picture as a good start. Fellowship is intimate association. We share activities, responsibilities and privileges. Disciples share life. More than that, we share *eternal* life, and the distinction is essential to true fellowship.

Disciples of Jesus hang out together, but fellowship is much more than that. Anybody can hang out with a few friends or even with strangers (say, at a sporting event or concert). But when the NT uses the term "fellowship" it speaks more technically about a deeper, more meaningful connection. What makes fellowship more is our union with Christ that is realized through his Spirit (Php 2:1). Just as the Spirit brings diverse gifts into one unified, functioning *body*, he also brings diverse people into one unified *fellowship*. As we saw earlier in this chapter, this fellowship is based on the fellowship we have with God the Son and God the father through faith in Jesus (1 Jn 1:3). The intimate relationship we have with God through Jesus works out into the intimate relationships we have with one another (v.7).

NT writers like Paul and John have helped us understand that fellowship is expressed in love and unity. Fellowship is based on the eternal life we have in common with other Christians, and that reality supersedes any differences that might normally divide us, whether ethnic, socio-economic, political, educational, cultural or any other division. The result is profound. People who would otherwise not likely hang out in the same circles come together in a community. This community reflects a bond far deeper than any other reality that might create community.

My family currently lives in Kansas City, a.k.a "Chiefs Kingdom." Late fall and winter are filled with "Red Fridays" and tailgating. Spend a few bucks for a ticket – and too many more for parking – and you can hang out at Arrowhead Stadium with a few of your closest friends and scream your lungs out. Now, that's a place where you can find blue collar and white collar, along with the upper social echelon in the climate-controlled box seats. There are people who never graduated high school alongside people with PhDs. There are all kinds of ethnic groups present. There are Christians and Muslims and Buddhists and atheists and agnostics. Kids of all ages from 9 months to 99 years. For all of these wearing Chiefs red, they probably feel a strong connection in this community. But this isn't fellowship. Not like what the Bible talks about.

Broaden the scope. Add the fans of the OTHER teams (Go Broncos!) who fill out the stadium. On one hand they are opposed, but on the other hand NFL fandom still unites them all in a kind of community. To that group you can add the millions at home watching on television. That's quite a diverse and, to some degree, unified community. But that is not fellowship.

What unites sports fans or music fans, or any other such group, is a triviality compared to what brings Christians together in fellowship. We are united by the eternal life and belonging that come through the Creator of everything who gave his own perfect and priceless life to pay for his Church with his blood. Our faith and trust in him bring us into fellowship with one another in a bond that is eternal and that is of immeasurable worth.

This reality that unites us in true fellowship demands expression that is proportionate to its own significance. No other associations can bring us such joy. No other affiliations require such commitment. No other community will endure like this one. How many fans jump ship after a few losing seasons? A true Christian could not treat the church so.

The NT is full of what many have called the "one-another's." There are dozens of statements that command Christians how to love one another in this fellowship. When a "one-another" fellowship is built, it looks like the Jesus we know from the Gospels, the way he lived with his disciples.

We cannot ignore a fellow Christian we don't particularly like, let alone avoid them altogether or, worse, assault them. We must love them. There can be a number of good reasons to leave one local church community for another, but among them cannot be a hatred for those for whom Christ died. Sadly, Christians are often known for infighting and church splits, but these are not characteristics of true fellowship. These struggles have plagued the Church since its birth recorded in Acts, but it is not God's doing, and it grieves him. We are called to love and unity.

This reminds us again of the gospel. We are a fellowship because of the work Christ completed in his death for sins and his resurrection. When we screw up this good fellowship he has provided for us, the remedy is the same as it is for any sin, for this too was nailed to the cross. We confess these wrongs and humbly obey his command to love one another.

Disciples of Jesus can hang out with each other just like any other group with something in common. Our spending time together is not inherently fellowship. But because of the one most important thing we have in common, any time we hang out can potentially be an expression of true fellowship. The difference depends not in the situation but in purpose and function. We may or may not express fellowship in a church worship service or at a barbeque or even a sporting event. The question is whether we are loving and serving one another to build each other up in the faith. If we are, then that is fellowship. Anything less may be fine, but it is not unique to a disciple of Jesus. Disciples are characterized by true fellowship with God that is expressed by loving fellowship with each other.

**Talk it over**

Together check out the "one-another's":

Be at peace with one another. (Mk 9:50)
Wash one another's feet. (Jn 13:14)
Love one another. (Jn 13:34[2x],35; 15:12,17; Rm 12:10; 13:8; 1 Thes 4:9; 1 Pt 3:8; 1 Jn 3:11,23; 4:7,11,12; 2 Jn 5)
Outdo one another in showing honor. (Rm 12:10)
Live in harmony with one another. (Rm 12:16)
No longer judge one another. (Rm 14:13)
Accept one another, just as Christ also accepted you. (Rm 15:7)
Instruct one another. (Rm 15:14)
Greet one another. (Rm 16:16; 1 Cor 16:20; 2 Cor 13:12; 1 Pt 5:14)
When you come together to eat, welcome one other. (1 Cor 11:33)
Have the same concern for each other. (1 Cor 12:25)
Serve one another through love. (Gal 5:13)
Watch out or, you will be consumed by one another. (Gal 5:15)
Let us not become conceited, provoking one another, envying one another. (Gal 5:26)
Carry one another's burdens. (Gal 6:2)
Bear with one another. (Eph 4:2; Col 3:13)
Be kind and compassionate to one another, forgiving one another. (Eph 4:32)
Speak to one another in psalms, hymns and spiritual songs. (Eph 5:19)
Submit to one another in the fear of Christ. (Eph 5:21)
In humility consider others as more important than yourselves. (Php 2:3)
Do not lie to each other. (Col 3:9)
Forgive one another. (Col 3:13)
Teach and admonish one another through psalms, hymns, and spiritual songs. (Col 3:16)
Increase and overflow with love for one another. (1 Thes 3:12)
Encourage each other. (1 Thes 4:18; 5:11; Heb 3:13; 10:25)
Build each other up. (1 Thes 5:11)
Watch out for one another to provoke love and good works. (Heb 10:24)

Don't criticize one another. (Jas 4:11)
Do not complain about one another. (Jas 5:9)
Confess your sins to one another and pray for one another. (Jas 5:16)
Be like-minded and sympathetic. (1 Pt 3:8)
Maintain constant love for one another. (1 Pt 4:8)
Be hospitable to one another. (1 Pt 4:9)
As each one has received a gift, use it to serve others. (1 Pt 4:10)
Clothe yourselves with humility toward one another. (1 Pt 5:5)

*Do any of these commands surprise or challenge you?*

*What persons or kinds of persons are hardest for you to live in fellowship with? Which are easiest?*

Discuss in your own words how fellowship is more than just hanging out together.

*Do you think most of your time with other Christians is spent exercising true fellowship, or in something less?*

**Pray**
Thank God for the fellowship you have with him through Jesus. Thank him for the fellowship he has provided with others in the Church. Ask him to help you love and serve others in true fellowship rather than simply hanging out or even avoiding them.

# Ch.8 Growing and Deepening in the Gospel Individually

In ch.7, we saw the variety of ways that disciples of Jesus grow and deepen in the gospel when they come together in large groups as well as in smaller groups or even one-on-one. These are interpersonal expressions of spiritual disciplines, and they are very important for the disciple's development as he becomes more and more like the amazing and wonderful Savior he loves and worships. Paul calls this being "conformed to the image of [God's] Son," Jesus Christ (Rm 8:29). We already saw how important the community of faith, our flesh-and-blood brothers and sisters in Christ, are to this process by which we are reshaped into Christ-likeness. The work is God's. As we have seen, he uses his Word, his Spirit and his people to chisel away what is fallen and worldly from us and to sculpt his work of art in us. We are each God's creative projects in Christ (Eph 2:10).

But, just as important as community is to our exercise in spiritual disciplines, much of our growth takes place in our own intentional self-discipline. We can easily see analogy in our contemporary physical fitness culture. One can certainly tap into health benefits by joining a fitness club or joining a Zumba class or the like. The community can offer much encouragement. Some even pay for personal trainers to go after really targeted results. But no club membership, no class, no trainer will have any significant or lasting result unless one is personally committed to self-discipline.

For a few seasons my wife and I watched the reality television show Biggest Loser. Contestants selected for the competition were all morbidly obese and looking for a life-changing transformation for health. For as long as they prevailed in the competition and remained on the show, they received every possible benefit to not only lose excess weight but to develop healthy habits for eating and exercising. They even received medical supervision and psychological counseling. All these benefits came to them in carefully crafted isolation, where they were insulated from many temptations that might lead them back into unhealthy patterns. Still, even with all these advantages, if the contestants did not maintain a personal commitment to their new healthy habits, they would fall back into the image they had before the show.

The same happens with our spiritual fitness. A church community, a Bible class, even a personal "trainer" committed to helping us one-on-one in our discipleship are all great and helpful tools, but they cannot replace our own personal commitment to self-discipline. Most of the things discussed in ch.7 that we do in community to grow in our faith are also things that we need to do in private as individuals.

Of course, some things like giving and serving require another person as a recipient for us to express the spiritual discipline. But many other things that we do together we can and should do alone. We must set aside times to read the Bible, to pray, to sing and worship God, and to confess sin to him. When we exercise spiritual disciplines alone as individuals, we can go into greater depth that can result in remarkably personal and intimate times with our Lord. Many people call these "quiet times." They will only happen with regularity, which we need, if one deliberately sets a time and place for them to happen. Often these times are best served by getting *alone* and getting *quiet*, that is alone with God and his Word. We should not only read God's Word but should *study* it, digging deep into the questions that come. In ch.6, I mentioned there are many tools to help with Bible study, including books on systematic theology and biblical commentaries. There are even free online resources to help you see things that are in the original biblical languages that are not always obvious in translation. One such resource is Lumina, found at netbible.org. This website includes a parallel resource of the biblical languages. Many other such resources are available.

As God's Spirit shows us something new, or gives a new exhilaration with a known truth, we dwell on that reality, or *meditate* on it. Unlike the transcendental meditation of pop culture, biblical meditation is not the emptying of the mind but the filling of the mind with biblical truth. If you read through the Psalms, you will get a good sense of what this kind of meditation is like. It is dwelling on God's character and his amazing works.

All these personal times of discipline and devotion are centered on God's Word because it is *life* to us (Ps 119:25,107; Jn 6:63,68; 1 Jn 1:1). It is living and effective to penetrate the depths of our hearts (Heb 4:12), and as we saw in ch.1, it teaches, rebukes, trains and instructs us in righteousness (2 Tm 3:16). Many people benefit from *journaling* in these times. This helps them reflect on what God has shown them, and it is a record that can be brought back to memory at future times, perhaps times of struggle or stumbling. Journaling may take several forms. Some disciples simply write in a paper journal. Some may reflect in a blog, which can extend the benefits to others who read the reflections, but, of course, most will not share the most intimate parts of those reflections. I personally have seen another form of spiritual journaling in my history. I am a musician and a songwriter, and I can trace some key pieces of my spiritual journey through songs I have written over the years.

Whatever the forms, the important thing about personal spiritual disciplines is that we find ways to drive the gospel into the deepest parts of our souls. We must be worshipers of God in private, or our public worship will be shallow, if not vacuous. The accumulation of these moments of self-discipline will be a depth and grounding in our faith that will carry us through times of doubt, testing and spiritual dryness.

One other spiritual discipline I have not yet mentioned was affirmed by Christ himself, who also took an occasion to help his disciples understand the proper way to observe it:

> Matthew 6:16–18
>
> 16 "Whenever you fast, don't be gloomy like the hypocrites. For they
> make their faces unattractive so that their fasting is obvious to people.
> Truly I tell you, they have their reward. 17 But when you fast, put oil on
> your head and wash your face, 18 so that your fasting isn't obvious to
> others but to your Father who is in secret. And your Father who sees in
> secret will reward you.

By saying, "whenever" Jesus is clearly operating under the assumption that fasting was a normal practice for his disciples under Judaism. Jesus himself prepared for his public ministry by fasting for 40 days alone in the wilderness before a time of testing by the devil (Mt 4:1-2; Lk 4:1-2). He also is then affirming that this practice would continue for the disciples as his followers. However, he issues a corrective against the way that fasting had become an abused spiritual discipline in his day. It had become a tool for getting noticed, a sign for others that the one fasting was "spiritual." Jesus instructed his disciples to not put on a show for others but rather to offer this sacrificial act secretly to the Father.

To be clear, fasting in the strictest sense mentioned in this passage is the deliberate denying oneself of food as a spiritual act of dependence and devotion to God. In fasting, we withhold *physical* nourishment to highlight our dependence upon God and his *spiritual* nourishment. It is common to take the occasion when the hunger pains hit to turn one's attention to seeking God in prayer, often about matters of great importance or when urgently seeking God's direction or powerful intervention in a crisis. But fasting is an effective discipline as a matter of regular frequency and in mundane circumstances as well. And many expand fasting to other forms. A pastor friend of mine once fasted from the NFL for a period of months. Someone else fasted from social media for a period of time. Some are medically unable to fast from all food but might fast from only certain types of food.

The point of fasting, whether in a strict or a less strict form, is that we are prioritizing the spiritual over the physical. We are showing our complete dependence upon God. And we are imposing self-discipline, not so we can proudly parade it before others but so we can honor God in private. This does not mean that fasting is undone if someone else knows about it. In fact, many times church leaders will challenge their congregants to join together in a period of fasting and prayer during a critical time for their church. Or a community of Christian friends may fast and pray for a special need. Still, even in such times of communal fasting, each person is offering this discipline as a personal act of worship to the Lord.

For many disciples – myself included – fasting is one of the easiest spiritual disciplines to undervalue and overlook. Of course, many non-Christians fast for physical reasons, but for the Christian fasting is one of the many ways that we draw closer to God through acts of personal devotion.

For a more in-depth look at all these spiritual disciplines, consider a resource like Don Whitney's book, Spiritual Disciplines for the Christian Life. Whether one is exercising these disciplines in private devotion to Christ or in community with other believers, these are things disciples do to draw closer to and become more like the Savior they worship.

**Talk it over**

*Which of the spiritual disciplines discussed are easiest for you to observe? Which do you find most challenging?*

*Have you ever fasted for spiritual reasons? If so, from what did you fast, and for how long?*

*Other than food, what other kind of fast would be a real sacrifice for you?*

*Have you ever kept a journal? Do you think some form of journaling would help you capture and reflect upon your private worship times?*

Discuss a biblical idea, verse or passage upon which you have meditated or could meditate.

# Ch.9 Enduring in a Hostile World

My wife and I currently live in Kansas City, *Kansas*. I emphasize Kansas because our city also sprawls into Missouri, and it is on that side of the border where lies the home of the Kansas City Chiefs. Most people around here wear a lot of red, and many go quite out of their minds whenever the Chiefs have a game. Of course, this is even more true with home games, when Arrowhead stadium fills up with rabid fans even as the parking lot has already been filled with tailgaters. If this has all been true for years and years of post-season failures and, more often, absences (and it has), then fandom around here has been on steroids now that Chiefs fans have their "messiah" in a brilliant and prolific young gun slinging quarterback, Patrick Mahomes. It is fun to watch.

But we didn't always live here. In our early years as a family, we lived in Denver. Specifically, we were there in the 1990's. That happened to be when Bronco fans were looking to their own hero, John Elway. Some of our earliest ministry experiences came there in Denver. Our son was born while we lived there. Our oldest daughter met her future husband there. Somehow, we Kansas natives over time became Broncos fans. (There are other allegiances in our family now, as we added other sons-in-law and grandkids.) Finally, the Denver Broncos overcame several empty trips to the title game and won two championships back-to-back in 1998 and 1999.

The Chiefs/Broncos rivalry is all in good fun within our family. But it has felt a little different on the occasions when I have attended a contest between these teams at Arrowhead. Wherever your seats, when you root for Denver in your Broncos swag surrounded by a sea of Chiefs fans in red, you do not feel welcome. Sure, many are polite enough. However, others give you a look that says something like, "Love your Broncos if you want...but I don't want to know about it, don't want to see it, don't want to hear it – not here in OUR house." Of course, a few others (especially a few beers into the game) may simply act as though they intend to rid you of all your offensive Broncos gear with no care to avoid bodily harm. Or worse.

We kind of expect this range of responses with football. People go a little crazy for about 17 weeks, or if their team is good, a few more. The same goes for basketball season, or an even longer baseball season. What about the national pride that rises up during a World Cup or the Olympics?

People can get pretty worked up over a game. Why would we expect any less with worldviews or faith?

As with sports, some are more rabid about those than others. Their fan swag might be a tee shirt or hat, or bumper stickers seem a popular choice. It is common to blend in political choices with worldviews and faith issues, so maybe add a button, sticker or pin to the swag. Beyond the swag, social media has given people a huge platform to spew their views. Pop culture develops around these things. Many people will call themselves Christians for all kinds of reasons that have nothing to do with personally knowing Christ. This is because there is still a place in the U.S. for Christian pop culture. For now. Many have already moved on to the secularization that already swept through Europe. They have found something more "enlightened," and now see Christians as naïve, foolish or worse, dangerous. Others reject a secular worldview but hold to a theism opposed to Christianity, or perhaps they opt for some supposedly transcendent spirituality that draws from Eastern religion or from native American influences.

Put all this together, and you have a reality of which every disciple of Jesus needs to be aware, especially a *new* disciple. Many people – in fact, probably most people – do *not* see Jesus as worthy of worship and devotion, especially as the *only* one worthy of these things. They do *not* see our God as the perfect Boss. And they don't much care for his Employees either. Many want to believe there is no Boss of them but themselves. So, when you try to explain that there is, in fact, a Boss, and that it is *not* them, they may well not be excited about this. What you call the "good news" of the gospel they do not see as good at all. The reality is that when you as a disciple of Jesus live out a vibrant, passionate life of holiness, that will generate a variety of responses from those around you. You hope and pray they will believe and trust Jesus too. But like with sports fans, many will politely coexist, some will disapprove and be bothered by your being there, and some might even aggressively cause you grief, or worse.

Now, it is one thing to have a disappointing reaction from someone when you share the gospel with them. That will happen. But it is another thing to have people predisposed against you, even when you haven't done anything to them or spoken a word to them. Jesus taught his disciples to expect this, not merely as a *possibility* but as a *norm*.

John 15:18–25

18 “If the world hates you, understand that it hated me before it hated
you. 19 If you were of the world, the world would love you as its own.
However, because you are not of the world, but I have chosen you out of
it, the world hates you. 20 Remember the word I spoke to you: ‘A servant
is not greater than his master.’ If they persecuted me, they will also
persecute you. If they kept my word, they will also keep yours. 21 But they
will do all these things to you on account of my name, because they don’t
know the one who sent me. 22 If I had not come and spoken to them, they
would not be guilty of sin. Now they have no excuse for their sin. 23 The
one who hates me also hates my Father. 24 If I had not done the works
among them that no one else has done, they would not be guilty of sin.
Now they have seen and hated both me and my Father. 25 But this
happened so that the statement written in their law might be fulfilled:
**They hated me for no reason.**

Jesus argues from the greater to the lesser (v.20): if the master endured hatred (and he obviously did), then we who serve him should expect no less. He makes this statement in the context of John’s Gospel that clearly shows throughout Jesus’ ministry the growing gap between Jesus and those who rejected him. The more he revealed himself through teaching and miraculous signs, the more polarized the responses. Revealing Jesus reveals sin (vv.22-24), and that makes many people mad. And the ones who feel the most threatened – like the religious leaders of Jesus’ day – may be capable of the worst forms of hate, even to the point of murder! While martyrdom (being put to death because you are a Christian) is not a likely cost for most of us in the West right now, it has been a reality for thousands and thousands of disciples since the 1st century. And the sober truth is that every disciple should expect that following Jesus will cost him or her. You’ve probably heard the saying, “We each have our own cross to bear.” This actually reflects the way Jesus talked about the cost of following him:

Matthew 16:24–28

> 24 Then Jesus said to his disciples, "If anyone wants to follow after me, let him deny himself, take up his cross, and follow me. 25 For whoever wants to save his life will lose it, but whoever loses his life because of me will find it. 26 For what will it benefit someone if he gains the whole world yet loses his life? Or what will anyone give in exchange for his life? 27 For the Son of Man is going to come with his angels in the glory of his Father, and then he will reward each according to what he has done. 28 Truly I tell you, there are some standing here who will not taste death until they see the Son of Man coming in his kingdom."

This self-denial of which Jesus speaks has much to do with the spiritual disciplines we discussed. It also has to do with enduring through various forms of persecution by a world that is hostile to Jesus. He did not want his disciples to be blind-sided and discouraged by those who would oppose them. So, he spoke frankly of the challenge. But he also offered hope. There is the hope of his coming reward for faithfulness and for his justice on those who mistreat his disciples (v.27). There is the hope that some will be converted through our witness (Jn 15:20c above). Ultimately, our hope, our encouragement is that we are united with Jesus in eternal life, and that cannot be taken from us (Jn 6:35-40; 43-47; 1 Jn 5:11-13; Rm 8:31-39).

The reality of persecution by a hostile world is such a prevalent NT theme that the Gospels and Acts trace out its early historicity. Then every book that follows deals instructively with it in some way, whether opposition from outside the church or division inside caused by false teachers. Even the dramatic Revelation recorded by John chimes in. For many, this bizarre book brings to mind cataclysmic judgments and the battlefield of Armageddon. The fact is, a key theme that ties the whole letter together is the challenging call for disciples to endure through persecution. Chapters 2-4 are exhortations to the churches of John's day to stand faithful to the truth in spite of opposition. Jesus himself – now glorified in heaven – speaks to the collection of churches with commendation and encouragement, but also with challenge and even rebuke. In these seven charges we find the language of endurance: to Ephesus, "Do the works you did at first" (2:5); to Smyrna, "Be faithful to the point of death" (v.10); to Pergamum, "Repent (of false teaching)" (v.16); to Thyatira, "Hold on to what you have until I come" (v.25); to Sardis, "Remember...what you have received and heard; keep it and repent [and be] alert" (3:3); to Philadelphia, "Hold on to what you have" (v.11); and to Laodicea, "Be zealous (for spiritual riches) and repent" (vv.18-19). Throughout these chapters we notice the perpetual need for the church to reform and be drawn back to center on Christ. And the church must dig in, determined to persevere for the sake of Christ. And then in the chapters that follow we are shown the height of persecution by the demonic world power that puts a huge number of believers to death. They follow Jesus in the most dramatic way possible.

That all feels too big and impossible to take in when I read it today in my comfortable office. It's not that different from the overwhelming feeling that can linger over someone after watching or reading an epic story like Tolkien's Lord of the Rings. You might be both exhilarated and exhausted, and only breathe out, "Whew!"

Many of Tolkien's characters were ambivalent toward Frodo's journey. They didn't know about their impending doom, their own slavery to an evil lord who wanted all power. They were unaware of the heir that helped Frodo and would one day rule on the throne. And many are equally ambivalent toward *your* journey, unaware of the devil who wants to destroy us all and steal God's glory, and unaware of the King who has already won the victory and will one day destroy the devil and sin and death forever.

But there were plenty who knew of the quest to save Middle Earth, and who worked hard against it. Sometimes working in secret, sometimes marching openly in war, they desperately tried to keep the King from his rightful throne and glory.

But *this* epic story, the victory of Jesus over sin and death – this is REAL. And the hostility is real. Satan accuses us day and night before God (Rv 12:10). He has opposed God and God-fearing people for all of human history (Gn 3; Job 1-2). He has opposed Jesus and his work since the Savior was born into this world (Lk 2:34). He continues to deceive and draw many people into his defiant activity ever since (1 Cor 16:9; Eph 2:1-2; Php 1:28; 2 Thes 2:4; 2 Tm 3:8; 4:15). And if all that weren't enough, we face the challenge of opposition within ourselves by our old fleshly desires (Rm 7:14-25; Gal 5:17).

This chapter is not meant as a downer, but as an eye-opener. The reality of a world that is hostile to true Christian faith (though, sadly, it often gets along quite well with empty pop-Christianity) does not in the least undermine the greater reality of our all-powerful Savior. He is greater than any opponent, just as John wrote when he discussed discerning and dealing with the opposition:

> 1 John 4:1–6
>
> **4** Dear friends, do not believe every spirit, but test the spirits to see
> if they are from God, because many false prophets have gone out into the
> world.
> 2 This is how you know the Spirit of God: Every spirit that confesses
> that Jesus Christ has come in the flesh is from God, 3 but every spirit that
> does not confess Jesus is not from God. This is the spirit of the antichrist,
> which you have heard is coming; even now it is already in the world.
> 4 You are from God, little children, and you have conquered them,
> because the one who is in you is greater than the one who is in the world.
> 5 They are from the world. Therefore what they say is from the world, and
> the world listens to them. 6 We are from God. Anyone who knows God
> listens to us; anyone who is not from God does not listen to us. This is
> how we know the Spirit of truth and the spirit of deception.

Jesus keeps his promise to be with us every step of the way (Mt 28:20b.) He gives us his peace (Jn 14:27). He lives in us, encouraging us and empowering us through his Spirit (Jn 14:15-17; 15:26-16:15). Our call to endure for the sake of Christ is important.

One of Jesus' earthly brothers made this clear. Jude apparently wanted to write a nice, casual letter celebrating the blessings of the salvation we Christians share, but instead found it necessary to write a short, urgent note compelling his readers to "contend for the faith that was delivered to the saints once for all" (v.3). How do we contend for the faith? By holding to the truth when some want to corrupt it (v.4). By building ourselves up in our faith:

Jude 20–23

20 But you, dear friends, as you build yourselves up in your most holy
faith, praying in the Holy Spirit, 21 keep yourselves in the love of God,
waiting expectantly for the mercy of our Lord Jesus Christ for eternal life.
22 Have mercy on those who waver; 23 save others by snatching them from
the fire; have mercy on others but with fear, hating even the garment
defiled by the flesh.

We endure for the glory of the one who is our strength and our righteousness in the holy presence of God:

Jude 24–25

24 Now to him who is able to protect you from stumbling and to make
you stand in the presence of his glory, without blemish and with great
joy, 25 to the only God our Savior, through Jesus Christ our Lord, be glory,
majesty, power, and authority before all time, now and forever. Amen.

We endure because we are more than fans. And he is more than a conqueror. He is the only God our Savior.

So, we know we should expect opposition, persecution, some kind of cost for being a faithful disciple. And knowing helps in advance to offset frustration, disillusionment or even despair. Further, knowing Christ's Spirit is with us, ministering to us and empowering us, gives us confidence and endurance. We build ourselves up in that security and pray for it.

One other thing I think is important to mention before thinking about the goal of all this. Do not see other people as the enemy. They are slaves, who are dead (Eph 2:1-2) and blind:

2 Corinthians 4:1–6

**4** Therefore, since we have this ministry because we were shown
mercy, we do not give up. [2] Instead, we have renounced secret and
shameful things, not acting deceitfully or distorting the word of God, but
commending ourselves before God to everyone's conscience by an open
display of the truth. [3] But if our gospel is veiled, it is veiled to those who
are perishing. [4] In their case, the god of this age has blinded the minds of
the unbelievers to keep them from seeing the light of the gospel of the
glory of Christ, who is the image of God. [5] For we are not proclaiming
ourselves but Jesus Christ as Lord, and ourselves as your servants for
Jesus's sake. [6] For God who said, "Let light shine out of darkness," has
shone in our hearts to give the light of the knowledge of God's glory in
the face of Jesus Christ.

Yes, other people may oppose you, even aggressively. But your call is to not give up (v.1), to minister mercy because you have been shown mercy, and to proclaim the light that has shone out of the darkness to you (vv.5-6). Love and pray for those that persecute you (Mt 5:44), that perhaps you might snatch them out of the fire of judgment (Jude 22-23). Don't see them as the enemy, but as ones under the enemy's dominion of darkness (Col 1:13). You have been rescued from this dominion. Pray and work that you may help them find that same rescue and come into the kingdom of the Son.

**Talk it over**

Read through Rv 1-2 and discuss the variety of ways the churches are commended, rebuked and challenged.

*In what ways does Jesus describe the rewards for those who endure in faithfulness to him?*

*What are some of the ways Christians are mistreated in the culture around you because of their faith?*

*Have you experienced any of these forms of persecution? If not, which kinds do you think you might expect at some point?*

*How do you tend to respond to opposition? Fighting back? Freezing? Withdrawing?*

*How will you need to prepare yourself to respond as you should when persecuted?*

**Pray**

Thank the Lord for enduring the worst persecution for your sake. Ask him for his strength to follow after him and carry whatever kind of "cross" you are called to endure. Ask on one another's behalf for this grace we need to endure faithfully. Make specific requests that come out of the discussion points above.

# Ch.10 The Goal of It all: Disciples Making Disciples

In Part One, we saw that everything finds its source and sustenance in God (Acts 17:28). We learned that because God is most excellent in every way, he offers his creatures his most excellent gift – to know him so that they might love and worship him. We understand from God's self-revelation that to know God is ultimately to know Jesus, the Eternal Son. God's revelation through his creation, through his ancient covenant people, through his written Word and through his Spirit all pointed to this Son he sent to reveal everything we can humanly know about God. More than that, because fallen humanity could never coexist with this perfectly holy God, the Son was sent to redeem us, to purify us to restore the fellowship God designed for us to have with him.

In Part Two, we explored how God has continued his self-revelation and his work of reconciliation through his people. We are those who follow Jesus the Son, justified by his perfect life and death for sin, and sanctified – transformed to be more and more like Jesus – by his Spirit and his Word in the loving fellowship of other Christians. So, while in Part One we learned who Jesus is, in Part Two we learned who his disciples are.

Then in Part Three we dug into the practical realities of what Jesus' disciples do. We saw that we proclaim this good news about Jesus wherever we go. We proclaim with God's Word, with our own personal testimony as witnesses about him and with holy lives that authenticate the real transforming power of knowing him. We also saw that we grow and deepen in the riches of the gospel by gathering together to proclaim it to one another. We serve one another in love as stewards of the vast variety of gifts God has given us. We also devote ourselves to growing and deepening through individual spiritual disciplines centered around the Bible and true worship of God.

Lastly, we saw that as disciples of Jesus we must prepare ourselves to endure testing and persecution in various forms and degrees by a world that is hostile to this Jesus whom we love and serve. We must be constantly reformed to the truths of the gospel and the biblical practices of true worship. We must be diligent to confess sin and maintain the love and unity of the church. We must hear our Savior's call to stand, to endure, to remain true to the end, no matter the cost. He has done this before us, and he walks with us as we follow him to the prize (Heb 12:1-2).

Why do we disciples do all this? Why spend all this energy and swim upstream against cultures that worship self or so many false gods?

The answers to those questions could fill many books but let me offer one reason for faithful discipleship, and two important benefits. Then I will close this resource with a final challenge that brings everything full circle in the goal of discipleship.

## The Reason for Discipleship, and Two Benefits

The benefits I'll mention cannot stand as reasons by themselves, but only as an outflow from this primary purpose. That primary purpose for faithfulness as disciples of Jesus has long been identified as the sole purpose for the existence of every created thing: *sola deo Gloria.* This Latin phrase owes to the Protestant Reformation, and it means that God alone is to receive the glory for everything. Paul in Php 2:9-11 explains how God's lifting up of Jesus the Son is for the explicit purpose of bringing God glory. We cooperate with God's (the Father's) purpose when we lift up the Son in lives of worship. Peter in 1 Pt 2:12 directly connects the faithful lives of Christians to the purpose of bringing God glory. Then, in ch.4, Peter boils a Christian code of conduct down into one summary purpose, "that God may be glorified through Jesus Christ in everything. To him be the glory and the power forever and ever. Amen."

The foundational principle of *sola deo Gloria* is rooted in God's creation of everything for his own pleasure:

> Revelation 4:11
>
> 11 Our Lord and God,
> you are worthy to receive
> glory and honor and power,
> because you have created all things,
> and by your will
> they exist and were created.

An ancient praise hymn recorded by Paul in Rm 11 captures the beauty of God's wisdom in creating all things for his glory:

Romans 11:33–36

33 Oh, the depth of the riches
both of the wisdom and of the knowledge of God!
How unsearchable his judgments
and untraceable his ways!
34 **For who has known the mind of the Lord?**
**Or who has been his counselor?**
35 **And who has ever given to God,**
**that he should be repaid?**
36 For from him and through him
and to him are all things.
To him be the glory forever. Amen.

Just as all things are "from him" so all things are "to him." That is, since God originates every created thing, it is for his glory. The very next thing Paul writes in this letter is that because of this truth we should "present [our] bodies as a living sacrifice... (for) this is our true worship" (12:1).

The follower of Jesus disciplines herself and endures hostility and testing so that she may bring God glory through Jesus Christ. Every disciple of Jesus has been shown "the immeasurable riches of God's grace" in him so that these riches might be displayed for all beings in heaven and earth for all ages (Eph 2:6-7).

From this primary and ultimate reason for faithful discipleship spring two benefits we receive as we commit to growing and maturing as a disciple of Jesus. We find fulfillment and joy in two categories.

First, as we learned in ch.7, God has chosen to pour his riches of grace into the fellowship of a loving church community that is united in fellowship with God the Father and Son (1 Jn 3-4). This is a powerful and emotive thing. People will join up with all kinds of groups just to feel like they belong to something bigger than themselves. Sociologists have long given this as a reason that many are pulled into street gangs. Many young people can be persuaded to do things they wouldn't otherwise do – including committing horrible crimes – just to earn the satisfaction of belonging to a group of people who they can identify with and who promise to "have their back." More common than this is the simple peer pressure that most young people feel to look or act certain ways to fit into their desired group, whether the jocks, the nerds, artistic types or some other clique. I referenced another form of seeking belonging when I talked about sports fans in ch.9. Belonging is a powerful desire that God built into us creatures. But it finds only one expression that glorifies God, and that is in the community of his people who find fulfillment in him.

Apart from God no one will ever find lasting community. People have long joked about finding community in hell – the eternal existence apart from God – offering a caricature of themselves partying with their old buddies and having more fun than God wants to allow in heaven. Jesus painted a very different picture. In Luke 16, he told of a rich man and a poor man who both died (vv.19-31). The rich man had whatever he wanted in this life, and though he knew about the poor man, he did nothing to help him. This abuse of the poor follows a pattern the OT prophets used to describe someone who did not love God. In the afterlife, the rich man is in torment, while the poor man is comforted. The rich man is separated, alone. He is not even named, though the poor man, Lazarus, is. Lazarus was carried by angels to Abraham's side. It seems he has found community. But the rich man has none. Their status after this life was not based on riches or poverty, but on whether they repented of sin and honored God (v.27-31). They learned how to do that from the prophets (including Jesus himself! vv.29-31). The rich man never did, and now he was alone and in torment. Lazarus apparently had, and now he had comfort and community, including hanging out with Abraham himself! Separation from God means darkness (Mt 25:30), destruction (Php 3:19; 2 Pt 3:7) and torment (Rv 20:10-15).

But in Christ, we find true community. All the walls we put up between us are broken down (Eph 2:11-22). Ethnicity, gender, social status, all distinctions over which we divide, are swallowed up in the unity of God's Spirit through Christ. This is not a loss of individuality but rather the bringing together of diversity into unity (the meaning of the term "university"). What a great benefit of following Christ for the glory of God!

We also find fulfillment and joy in an even more personal sense. The second benefit is internal. We are personally at peace with God, and we find joy in the fulfillment of his purpose in creating us. We are like a pot made for honor (2 Tm 2:20-21). In Christ we have been purified and set apart for honoring God. In living for God, we are discovering and fulfilling our purpose for existing!

This is another powerful craving built into every person. We all are pulled to an awareness and sense of a reality greater than us (Ecc 3:11; Rm 1:18-20). Many suppress the truth about this sense and seek to define their own sense of purpose (vv.21-25). But we who are disciples of Jesus have heard and believed the gospel, and it has saved us and given us life (vv.16-17)! That sense of purpose now makes sense. As we live for God's glory, we are being fulfilled personally.

Living for God's glory, finding joy and fulfillment personally and among the community of the church, experiencing peace and fellowship with God himself – through all this, we come to the goal of our discipleship.

## The Goal of Discipleship

The goal of discipleship is to perpetuate the cycle of disciple-making until Jesus comes. In other words, the goal is to make disciples that make disciples that make disciples – and so on. In Mt 28:18-20, we get a vivid picture of the disciple maker as one who transfers disciple-making "DNA" into others.

> 18 Jesus came near and said to them, "All authority has been given to
> me in heaven and on earth. 19 Go, therefore, and make disciples of all
> nations, baptizing them in the name of the Father and of the Son and of
> the Holy Spirit, 20 teaching them to observe everything I have
> commanded you. And remember, I am with you always, to the end of the
> age."

The command to "make disciples" has imbedded in it the modifier "teaching them to observe everything I have commanded you." This means that making disciples means teaching those disciples to make disciples. We pass on the command of Jesus to the disciples we are making, so their command also is to make disciples. And they pass the command on to those disciples that they will make. The heritage of disciple-making through the power of the gospel has carried through two millennia of generations. To you.

You too are called to make disciples that will make other disciples, even as you continue to grow and deepen in your own faith. This process of multiplication is the method God has chosen to use to bring salvation and eternal life to those he is calling to himself. So, while everyone with whom we share the gospel will not believe, we share it with everyone we can so that those who *will* believe *can*. Paul told Timothy this was his reason for sharing the gospel at any cost (including imprisonment and martyrdom):

2 Timothy 2:8–10

> 8 Remember Jesus Christ, risen from the dead and descended from
> David, according to my gospel, 9 for which I suffer to the point of being
> bound like a criminal. But the word of God is not bound. 10 This is why I
> endure all things for the elect: so that they also may obtain salvation,
> which is in Christ Jesus, with eternal glory.

Elsewhere Paul explained that we must be faithful for our part in this disciple-making process, because God has decreed that disciples will not be made any other way:

Romans 10:14–17

> 14 How, then, can they call on him they have not believed in? And how
> can they believe without hearing about him? And how can they hear
> without a preacher? 15 And how can they preach unless they are sent? As
> it is written: **How beautiful are the feet of those who bring good**
> **news.** 16 But not all obeyed the gospel. For Isaiah says, **Lord, who has**
> **believed our message?** 17 So faith comes from what is heard, and what
> is heard comes through the message about Christ.

There are more disciples God is calling to himself, to faith, to follow his Son, Jesus. He has decided to call them through your proclamation of the gospel. Then when they believe the message you proclaim, that is not the *end* of evangelism but rather the *beginning* of discipleship. Far too many have had too small a view of Jesus' Great Commission, seeing evangelism itself (proclamation of the gospel) as the finish line rather than a starting gate. The goal is not merely to get someone to make a confession about Jesus and repeat some verbal prayer. The goal is discipleship, and Jesus defined that as "teaching [someone] to observe everything I have commanded you." What Paul said in Rm 10:9-10 is true:

Romans 10:9–10

> [9] If you confess with your mouth, "Jesus is Lord," and believe in your heart that God raised him from the dead, you will be saved. [10] One believes with the heart, resulting in righteousness, and one confesses with the mouth, resulting in salvation.

However, in this brief statement Paul is speaking only of the nature of saving faith. He is not discussing the broader, ongoing process of disciple-making which Jesus commanded. In fact, much of what we understand about that ongoing process of growth we learn from Paul. His basic *modus operandi* in his letters is to write about the doctrinal foundation of our faith and then to move to practical challenges to grow and mature in that faith.

Likewise, in the earliest days of the church, Peter preached the gospel and called people to repent and believe in Jesus for the forgiveness of sins (Acts 2:38). But for those who responded in belief, this repentance led to ongoing discipling as the new believers "devoted themselves to the apostles' teaching, to the fellowship, to the breaking of bread, and to prayer" (v.42), things we discussed in chs.8 & 9 that disciples do. We see the result was a tight-knit community of fellowship, service and joy (vv.44-47). These disciples kept reproducing as we see in the last statement of that chapter, "Every day the Lord added to their number those who were being saved."

That is the goal of every disciple. To keep adding to the number of disciples. As we do, we keep teaching new disciples so that they both learn biblical truth and live out godly behaviors, observing the commands of Jesus. Then those disciples make new disciples, and they teach them biblical truth and godly behaviors. God continues to be glorified by more and more of those he has called to himself in Jesus. More are added to the fellowship. More finally find fulfillment and joy in the purpose for which they were created, to glorify God forever.

That is the goal of this resource. These pages barely summarize, barely scratch the surface of this glorious calling we have been given, to make disciples. My hope is that it has been useful in some way for disciple-making in your case. More than that, I challenge you to answer this call, whether with this or some other resource, but always by the Word of God, empowered by his Spirit. Make disciples. To some extent, at the very least by going through these pages in whatever setting, someone has been discipling you. Answer the call to do the same. Make disciples for the glory of God!

**Talk it over**
*Whatever the setting, how did God bring you to go through this resource?*

*What was God's purpose for bringing disciple-making to your attention now?*

*Regardless of your role in going through this study, how has God blessed you through the time and effort spent?*

*How does your own discipling continue now?*

*To whom will you commit to help disciple?* Name names, if possible.

**Pray about it**
Give thanks to God for his working in your times together in considering discipleship. Thank him for the one(s) with whom you have been going through these truths. If God has shown you someone you should approach about discipling, then ask him to direct that opportunity and fill it with his presence and power. If you do not yet know to whom he will send you to help challenge for growth, ask him to show you someone to approach. Ask God for boldness to continue to proclaim the gospel to those who have not yet believed in Jesus, for that is the beginning of discipleship.

# Other Books by this Author

Benjamin Gum has also written several Bible studies in workbook format, including the following: **The Revelation of Jesus Christ: A Journey through the Apocalypse Guided by Its Purpose, Function and Goal; Job: The Cry of the Righteous Sufferer** and **Hebrews: The Superior Son and the Exhortation to Endure**. Gum has also written **Skinny Jeans Fat Shoes**, a challenge aimed primarily at worship leaders.

www.ingramcontent.com/pod-product-compliance
Lightning Source LLC
LaVergne TN
LVHW041256080426
835510LV00009B/758

* 9 7 8 1 7 3 4 4 9 6 2 0 8 *